INTERNATIONALIZATION OF HIGHER EDUCATION

An Aspect of India's Foreign Relations

INTERNATIONALIZATION OF HIGHER EDUCATION

An Aspect of India's Foreign Relations

Kavita A. Sharma

GYAN PUBLISHING HOUSE
New Delhi-110002

Internationalization of Higher Education :
An Aspect of India's Foreign Relations

Rs. 500

ISBN : 978-81-212-1006-5

Published in 2008 in India by
Gyan Publishing House
5, Ansari Road, Darya Ganj
New Delhi - 110002
Phones : 23261060, 23282060, Fax : 23285914
E-mail: books@gyanbooks.com

Laser Typesetting at : Master Computers, Delhi
Printed at : Singhal Print Media, Delhi

Contents

Abbreviations for the Institutions Listed in Appendices IV & VI

ACME	College, Hyderabad
ACOU	Arts College, Osmania University
AIIMS	All Indian Institute of Medical Sciences
AIIS	American Institute of Indian Studies, New Delhi
AMC	Assam Medical College, Dibrugarh
BHU	Banaras Hindu University
BIMS	Bahadur Institute of Management Sciences University of Mysore
CDAC	Center for Development of Advanced Computing, Mohali
CFTR	Central Food Technology Research Institute, Mysore
CT	College of Insurance
CIEFL	Central Institute of English and Foreign Languages, Hyderabad
CIH	Confederation of Indian Horticulture
CIH	Central Institute of Hindi, Agra
CITD	Central Institute of Tool Design
CMC	Christian Medical College, Ludhiana
CMR	CMR Institute of Management Studies, Bangalore
CPU	Christ PU College, Bangalore
DOON	Doon International School
DU	Delhi University
EDI	Entrepreneurship Development Institute of India, Ahmedabad
EDI	Entrepreneurship Development Institute of India
FC	Ferguson College, University of Poona
FMS	Faculty of Management Studies
GCM	Government College for Men, Punjab University, Chandigarh
GLC	The Government Law College, Mumbai
GMC	Grant Medical College
IAMR	Institute of Applied Manpower Research, Delhi

IBB	Institute of Bio-informatics & Biotechnology, University of Pune
ICDS	Integrated Child Development Services
ICM	Institute of Credit Commercial Management, Delhi
IDS	Institute of Development Studies, Mysore
IIM	Indian Institute of Management, Bangalore
IIMC	Indian Institute of Mass Communication, Delhi
IIRS	Indian Institute of Remote Sensing
IIT	Indian Institute of Technology, Madras
ITT	Indian Institute of Technology, New Delhi
IKS	Indra Kala Sangeet Vishwavidyalaya, New Delhi
ISI, Kolkata	Indian Statistical Institute, Kolkata
JB Campus	J. B. Campus, Bangalore University, Bangalore
JNU	Jawaharlal Nehru University, New Delhi
KC College	Kishanchand Chellaram College, Mumbai
KMC	Kasturba Medical College, Mangalore
LC	Loyala College.
MAHE	Manipal Academy of Higher Education
MCODS	Manipal College of Dental Sciences, Mangalore
MCOPS	Manipal college of Pharmaceutical Sciences
MIT	Manipal Institute of Technology
MPS	M. P. Shah Medical College, Jamnagar
MSRMC	M S Ramaiah Medical College, Bangalore
MSU	MS University of Baroda
NCRB	National Crime Records Bureau, Delhi
NIESBUD	National Institute for Entrepreneurship and Small Business Development, NOIDA, Campus
NIFM	National Institute of Financial Management, Faridabad
NIFM	National Institute of Financial Management, Faridabad
NIIT	National Institute of Information Technology, Delhi
NISIET	National Institute of Small Industry Extension Training Hyderabad
NLS	National Law School of India, Bangalore
NWC	Nowrjee Wadia College, Pune
OU	Osmania University.
PGI	Post Graduate Institute, Chandigarh
PUC	Punjab University, Chandigarh
RMC	Ramaiha Medical College
SIBIT	Shriram Institute of Business and Information Technology, Gurgaon, Haryana
SPU	Sardar Patel University, Gujarat
STS	Starex International School
UOP	University of Pune
VIT	Vishwakarma Institute of Technology, Pune
VRI	Vrindavan Research Institute
YM College	Yashwantrao Mohite College of Arts, Science and Commerce, Pune

Foreword

Dr. Kavita Sharma's study, *Internationalisation for Higher Education: Role of Education Sector*, examines an important facet of India's foreign and education policy. Its central thesis, that the flow of ideas, the internationalization of India's education sector, and a broader attention to the dynamics of soft power, can be an extraordinary instrument for our foreign policy is extremely timely. The study is full of wonderful empirical materials: from the history of India's engagement with the broader world in the field of education to a mapping of various contemporary strategies for internationalization of education. Dr. Sharma is very alive to the possibilities of internationalization of the Indian education system. But she also gives due attention to the formidable limits placed on India's education system as currently run and constituted. She also does something that studies of education and the external sector have rarely done: examine the ways in which the Indian Diaspora can be a catalyst in internationalizing the Indian system. Readers will find deeply interesting data on the composition of the international student body in India, and the possibilities that remain to be tapped in this sector. Dr. Sharma has examined all kinds of institutions from universities to government run cultural bodies, and has adopted a range of methodologies, from using published data to extensive field work and interviews. The result is an engaging book.

There is very little doubt that if India gets its policies and institutions right, it can become a major global hub of Higher Education. It will have to improve the quality of its public institutions, get its regulatory regimen for private and not-for-profit players in order, and encourage the kinds of investment that not only enhance the quality at the top, but also increase the median quality of Indian institutions. Only then will India be in a position to take major advantage of the opportunities that Dr. Sharma has outlined. There are many intrinsic reasons to push for reforms that enable India to exploit this opportunity. Dr. Sharma has convincingly argued that in the end, there is no force more powerful than the power of ideas. It is high time India woke up to this fact.

Dr. Sharma conducted this study while associated with The Center for Policy Research under a grant by the Ministry of External Affairs. We are grateful to the MEA for making this study possible and to Dr. Sharma for executing it.

Pratap Bhanu Mehta

Preface

The thought that education can be a valuable tool in creating understanding, cooperation and goodwill among nations, besides also bringing economic benefits, came to me during my stay in Vancouver, Canada where my husband, J.C. Sharma was posted as Consul General at the peak of the Khalistan movement. I had an intimate contact with the University of British Columbia as I was myself a student doing my Masters in Law at that time. I realized the extent of misinformation, disinformation and lack of information among students of the Indian community and among their peers in other communities that contributed to the formation of their views, responses and thereby actions. So much so, that the Indian community contributed to establish a chair of Sikh studies at the University of British Columbia.

Another aspect of the University system that I realized there was that they encouraged student diversity as a positive factor on the campuses. Back home, I was amazed at the indifference in our own system to diversity and often even resistance to it. A further look into the matter was triggered by the experience of and research into the North American higher education system and by analysing the responses of the Indian diasporic community to events back home. It resulted in a book and a couple of articles on how the education sector can actually help in building bridges and how it can thereby prepare the ground for creating an understanding about a country's position on various issues. It was revealing how the USA had instituted Study Abroad Programme and also had used education as an intrinsic and vital factor in public diplomacy. The continuing interest has led to this study.

The presentation is divided into four sections. The first deals with the power of ideas and their ability to mould thought and action. The second section explores education as an instrument of policy. The case of America and India is discussed. The third section concentrates on India to show that there has been an understanding of this aspect of education but it has not been properly foregrounded and implemented. The fourth section tries to fathom the responses of the students themselves who are currently studying in India or are alumni. It is by no means a rigorous statistical analysis but only indicative of general trends. Based on that, some recommendations have been made.

Apart from other things, this has been an exciting adventure into getting a glimpse of our own higher education system first hand experientially. It was a valuable education in itself. Political uncertainties prevented me from visiting countries like Nepal and Bangladesh but having done this study, I am convinced that a more detailed study needs to be done on our educational ties with our neighbours, the implications and prospects. It would be another adventure worth embarking upon.

Kavita A. Sharma

Acknowledgements

First and most important, thanks are due to my husband J.C. Sharma, former Secretary, Ministry of External Affairs for having inspired, planned and gone all out to help in completion of the project. I acknowledge with gratitude the Ministry of External Affairs for making the funds available to make this study possible and the Centre for Policy Research for providing a platform from which it could be conducted. Professor Charan Wadhwa and Professor Bhanu Pratap Singh have encouraged and facilitated on every occasion.

Thanks are also due to the following: Shri Chandrachur Singh from Hindu College for his valuable help and contribution in researching and writing; to Shri Kanwar Manjit Singh and Shri R.K.Singh for help in providing logistic support during my field study. Dr. Sudhir Kapoor, Reader in the Department of Statistics from Hindu College for his help for providing statistical material. My grateful thanks to the various institutions including Indian missions abroad, faculty members and colleagues for helping with the field study particularly in making contact with students both current and alumni to answer the questionnaire. The institutions whose help I gratefully aknowledge are :

Manipal Academy of Higher Education, Manipal Institute of Technology, Manipal; Manipal College of Dental Surgery, Mangalore, University of Mumbai; H.R. College of Commerce, Mumbai, University of Baroda; Apex Education Foundation, Pune; Kasturba Medical College, Mangalore; Central Institute for English as a Foreign Language, Hyderabad, Hemchandracharya North Gujarat University, Patan, International Centre Sardar Patel University, Gujarat; Gujarat University Navrangpura, Ahmedabad, Director of the International Programme, Bangalore; Director of International Programme, Mysore; University Foreign Relations Office, Osmania University, Hyderabad; Centre For the Study of Indian Diaspora, Hyderabad; Nizam College, Osmania University, Hyderabad; University of Mumbai, Vidyanagri, Santacruz, Mumbai; Symbiosis, Senapati Bapat Road, Pune; St. Xavier's College, Mumbai, Hyderabad(Sind); National Collegiate Board, DW Road, Mumbai; Nowrosjee Wadia College, Pune; B.M.S. Educational Trust, Bull Temple Road, Bangalore; Educational Consultant International Bharati Vidyapeeth, LBS Marg, Pune; Department of Politics and Public Administration, University of Pune; Sardar Patel University, Gujarat; National Law School of India University, Nagarbhavi, Bangalore; Faculty of Industrial Design, Ahmedabad; Office of the Assistant Labour Commissioner, Ahmedabad; University of Agricultural Sciences, Bangalore; Office of the Assistant Labour Commissioner, Vadodara; Fergusson College, Pune; H.R.College of Commerce and Economics; National Institute of Design, Paldi Ahmedabad; Melaka-Manipal Medical College, Malaysia; Faculty of Social Administration Thammasat University, Bangkok, Thailand; the University of Fiji, Fiji; Department of Politics and Public Administration, University of Pune; Department of Agricultural Sciences, Bangalore.

Thanks are particularly due to our missions in Thailand, Malaysia, Mauritius, Fiji and Zambia. Thanks are due to my friend Ms. Indu Ram Chandani, Ms. Jehanara Wasi and Mr. Sitakanta Mishra for their help in copy editing and valuable suggestions. Further I wish to acknowledge the following for secretarial help and logistic support without which the project could never have been completed: Shri T.C.Arora, Smt. Rajesh Sharma, Shri Dinesh Kumar and Shri Dinesh Singh. There are many others who have lent support in various ways and to whom I am grateful.

Kavita A. Sharma

1

Power of Ideas

Introduction

The premise of the study is that if India has to emerge as a global leader, it has to gain preeminence in the field of education. It cannot compete with the developed world in military might. Nor can it acquire the economic muscle equal to theirs in spite of its fast growing economy in the near future. Although it has a sizeable educated and skilled middle class, as all social indicators show there is still a long way to go before India can be counted amongst developed countries. So what is the field in which India can gain preeminence and be counted as a significant global actor? It is the development of human resource. Thanks to the groundwork done immediately after independence in establishing institutions for scientific, technical, agricultural, medical education apart from liberal university education and the subsequent rapid increase in the education system, India has emerged as a developer of skilled human resource. What used to be lamented as brain drain is now seen as human capital. Developing countries too look to India for help in developing their own human resource. This was understood in post-independence India and it led to the establishment of institutions like the Indian Council of Cultural Relations (ICCR).[1] The First Education Commission of India, popularly known as the Kothari Commission, (1964-1966) stated that "the destiny of India" was "being shaped in her classrooms."[2]

The Education Commission was also emphatic that knowledge was international and that there could be no barriers to obtaining it from anywhere in the world. But India could not forever remain at the receiving end of the pipeline. It had to make its own contribution as an intellectual and cultural equal in the human endeavours to extend the frontiers of knowledge. This, as the Kothari Commission pointed out, required a large-scale programme for the discovery and development of talent and the creation of centres of excellence in higher education that could compare favourably with the best in the world.[3] It was through education that India could grow and find its place in the comity of nations by transforming its society.

Education has an immense power to shape the minds of human beings. How important and powerful this is can be seen from the UNESCO Charter that begins with the statement: "Since wars begin in the minds of men, it is in the minds of men that the defences of peace must be constructed."[4] It is through education that ideas spread and are carried across the world. This is the way Indian culture and knowledge made an impact in South East Asia, Central Asia and the Far East. In the contemporary world, too, the power of ideas is felt beyond the national boundaries. Rapid means of communication and transportation in the second half of the twentieth century made it easier to work and settle in different parts of the world wherever there were better professional and material opportunities. The development of information technology has made almost instant communication possible. This has created plural societies within national boundaries with multiple loyalties and identities. They are loosely termed diasporic communities and governments often try to make their positions known and highlighted through them in the countries where they live. The spread of democracy has empowered individuals who come together to form associations based on commonalty of interest. These influence policy and the decision-making of governments. No issue has remained a domestic concern. Since there is a plurality of communities spread across different parts of the world, the impact is felt globally. The development and widespread use of information technology ensures that information can be disseminated and accessed quickly and advocacy groups in different parts of the world can be activated at the touch of a button.

Several questions arise. How can education be used to create a voice for India in the comity of nations? What was the impact of Western education in India through the colonial experience? Why did America gradually replace UK as the education destination for aspiring Indians? And what were its consequences ? Why and how did India try to make its educational facilities available to several developing countries particularly in the erstwhile British colonies? Can education be used to strengthen the bonds of the large Indian diaspora with India and with each other? What are the reasons for the current interest of the educational institutions of developed countries in India? To what extent are Indian educational institutions aware of the impact they can have by internationalizing their education system and campuses? What would be the significance of this on India's external relations? Finally, what policy decisions can be taken in this regard and how can they be implemented?

Organization of States

The world is divided into separate territorial political communities, or sovereign states that profoundly affect the way people live. Together these states form an international system that is global in extent. At present there are almost two hundred independent states and everybody, with very few exceptions, not only lives in one of them and is its citizen, but increasingly, a citizen of more than one state. So virtually everyone is connected to one state or the other and via that state to the international system that affects his or her life in many more ways than the person may be fully aware of. States are independent of each other being sovereign, but they are not isolated or insulated from each other. On the contrary, they adjoin each other and affect each other. For mutual benefit, therefore, they must find ways to coexist and interact. In dealing with the rest of the world, states have to try and achieve their objectives and aspirations in consonance with the imperatives of the contemporary. To that extent they formulate policies and processes not only in keeping with their own ethos and societal milieu but also with due regard to the international order.

The state system therefore has a distinctive way of organizing political life on earth and it has deep historical roots. Whether it was the Greco-Roman system or the Indus Valley Civilization, or for that matter, the modern nation-state that emerged through the Treaty of Westphalia in 1648, specific strategies and policies have always been tried by them to fulfil their aspirations but mindful of others and their responses. An understanding of strategies and objectives of other states is also important to uphold certain basic values such as security, freedom, order, justice, and prosperity.

It is generally assumed that states should, and will, protect the value of security, which means protecting their citizens from internal and external threats. States will also try to build military power so that they coexist and deal with each other without being intimidated or subjugated. To achieve this end, many states enter into military alliances with other states to increase their national security. Various techniques, from the balance of power to collective security, have been employed by states for this purpose. Security is obviously of paramount importance. This kind of concern was represented in what is called Realism in international relations. It was based on the assumption that the state is the most important actor in international relations and that the diplomatic-strategic relations of states are the core of actual international politics.[5]

Hans J. Morgenthau [6] has been the best exponent of such a perspective as he tried to fuse national interest and power. However, through the 1960s and 1970s these assumptions seemed less plausible. Perhaps the resolution of the Cuban Crisis and the inability of the USA to turn its obvious advantage in terms of power into results in the Vietnam War were the reason behind such thinking. As the threat of the Cold War turning into a widespread conflict decreased, the significance of international social and especially, economic relations increased.

The issue of security has now been taken over by that of prosperity. This change has been highlighted by Robert Keohane and Joseph Nye.[7] They have demonstrated the importance of non-state actors and the extent to which these affect lives of people in distant parts of the world. Later, the two authors proposed that complex interdependence is a significant factor in international relations together with realistic self-interest.[8] Complex interdependence assumes multiple channels of access between societies and that force is of low salience. Further, there is no hierarchy of issues and any issue-area could be at the top of the international agenda at any particular time. For example, people expect their governments to adopt appropriate policies to encourage high employment, low inflation, steady investments, the uninterrupted flow of trade and commerce and so on. Since national economies are rarely isolated from each other, states have to respond to the international economic environment to not only maintain but also enhance the national standard of living. Economic interdependence has thus become a striking feature of contemporary international relations.

Since the world has become smaller and the states more interdependent than ever before, there is a much greater interest in each other's culture, language, and way of life. This is because in a shrunken world people necessarily have to interact with each other in increasingly greater spheres such as trade, ecology, environment, and human rights. International treaties and conventions have started creating world regimes not only in these areas but also in fields as private as marriage, divorce, child custody, maintenance, and inheritance. For example, abandoned wives by NRI husbands has become a problem that needs urgent attention and will require India to become part of bilateral or multilateral treaties in a sphere which would not have required serious participation even a few years ago.

Another important factor that has enhanced people power is the spread of democracy. As Friedman points out, two major events have been responsible for this. One is the end of the Cold War, which has also been a struggle between two economic systems—capitalism and communism. Second is the fall of the Berlin Wall on November 9, 1989.[9] Now there is only one system and everyone has had to orient and adapt to it one way or another. Henceforth, more and more economies would be governed in consonance with interests, demands, and aspirations of the people, that is, from ground up rather than by planning from top down. With the spread of democracy, regulated or centrally planned economies have become an idea of the past.

The issue of Democratic Peace has become vital. The democratic peace theory, or liberal peace theory, or simply democratic peace, holds that democracies—usually, liberal democracies—never, or almost never, go to war with one another.[10] Thus the stage has been set for an open system of international relations where people and public opinion is important in government decision-making and action. Therefore, culture, norms and attitudes of societies are also significant in determining the path that nations can take to pursue their national interests.

Soft Power

According to UNESCO, "Culture comprises the whole complex of distinctive spiritual, material, intellectual, and emotional features that characterize a society or social group. It includes not only the arts and letters, but also modes of life, the fundamental rights of the human being, value systems, traditions and beliefs."[11] If we accept this definition, educational institutions, organizations, and instruments must necessarily play an important part in creating an understanding of a nation's culture because education is nothing but the ability and training of the mind to receive, comprehend, use, and disseminate ideas. And ideas are powerful because they are seductive.

Once the individual got empowered and became collaboratively aligned through ideas, businesses, skills, and opportunities, it led to further flattening of hierarchies, to use Friedman's phrase, in almost all areas spawning self-arranging collaborative communities.[12] Hence people-to-people interaction cannot now be ignored by any government because the world has had to shift from a primarily vertical command and control value creation model to an increasingly horizontal and collaborative creation model. In such a world co-option and collaboration are extremely important for a country to achieve its objectives and have a say in the comity of nations. The twin objectives of co-option and collaboration must become essential features through which foreign policy objectives have to be accomplished.

Foreign policy can be described as a system of activities by states for changing the behaviour of other states and for adjusting their own activities to the international environment. It is a policy pursued by a nation in its dealings with other nations, designed to achieve national objectives. Foreign policy has, as Utpal Bannerji points out, a three-pronged approach.[13] It tacitly accepts another country's position, understands its point of view, and dialogues with it to make its own position and approach acceptable. In today's world this cannot be done only at the government level. The understanding has to be people-to-people. Hence, the importance of what Joseph Nye calls the "soft power".[14]

The dictionary meaning of power is the "capacity to do things". At the most general level, it means the ability to get the outcomes one wants. It also means the capacity to affect the behaviour of others to make those things happen. So more specifically, power is the ability to influence the action of others to get the desired result. But there are several ways to affect the behaviour of others. They can be coerced with threats or induced by payments or they can be convinced and co-opted to do what one wants them to do. The exercise of power through attraction rather than through coercion or payments is termed by Joseph Nye as soft power. He first developed this concept of soft power in *Bound to Lead* in 1999 and returned to it in 2001 in *The Paradox of American Power*.[15]

In *Bound to Lead,* Nye discussed the nature and exercise of power. After pointing out the limits of military and economic power, Nye said that a country could achieve the outcomes it wanted in world politics because other countries wanted to follow it or had agreed to a system that produced desired effects. In this sense, it is as important to set the agenda and structure the situation in world politics, as it is to get others to change in that particular situation. This aspect of power, that is getting others to want what you want, may be called indirect or co-optive power.[16]

Much earlier, Steven Lukes talked of the three dimensions of power in which the third dimension was ideological in nature. "Is it not", he asked,

> the supreme and most insidious exercise of power to prevent people, to whatever degree, from having grievances by shaping their perceptions, cognitions and preferences in such a way that they accept their role in the existing order of things, either because they can see or imagine no alternative to it, or because they see it as natural and unchangeable, or because they value it as divinely ordained and beneficial?[17]

According to Lukes, one-dimensional power consists of decision-making exercised in formal institutions and measured by the outcomes of the decisions made. It involves "a power of behaviour in the making of decisions on issues over which there is an observable conflict of (subjective) interests, seen as express policy preferences, revealed by political participation."[18] Two-dimensional power adds agenda-setting to decision-making and informal influences to the formal institutions of one dimensional power. The techniques used by two-dimensional power structures are influence, inducement, persuasion, manipulation, authority, threat, and direct force. Its measure is the extent of informal influence. The three-dimensional power includes aspects of one and two but also shapes preferences through values, norms, and ideologies. All social interaction involves power because ideas operate behind all language and action. It is not obviously measurable and its existence can only be inferred. For example, ideas and values ground all social activities whether they are religious or secular. Then there are factors like self-interest for economic gain or political ideologies that inform policy without being explicit. Very often these become routine and become taken for granted societal norms that are not consciously thought of.[19]

Alvin Toffler, too discusses the changing nature of power in *Powershift*.[20] According to him there are three main kinds of power–violence, wealth, and knowledge. All other kinds of power are variations of these three. Each successive power is more flexible than the previous one. Violence can only be used negatively to punish or coerce. Wealth can be used both negatively and positively; negatively by withholding money and positively by advancing or spending money,[21] Knowledge, too, can be used both negatively and positively like wealth, but additionally, it can also be used transformatively. For example, knowledge of agriculture can be used to ensure that everyone develops the capacity to supply food to himself and his family. Shared identities because of the commonality of religious or political philosophies bring about alliances among nations. Knowledge can be used for tactical or strategic superiority in intelligence or information gathering.[22]

Nye returned to the idea of co-optive power in the *Paradox of American Power* in 2001 where he observed that military and economic power were examples of hard command power that could be used to induce others to change their positions. Hard power rests on inducements or threats. But there is also an indirect way to exercise power. A country tries to obtain its desired objectives by attracting other countries which admire its values and want to emulate it or aspire to its levels of prosperity and openness. "This aspect of power—getting others to want what you want," says Nye, "I call soft power. It co-opts people rather than coerces them."[23]

In 2004, Nye analysed the concept even further and with greater urgency after the September 11 disaster in *Soft Power*.[24] This is because he felt that after the Cold War, America had neglected soft power and so its point of view was not being appreciated the way it should be. It had created anti-Americanism leading to the paradox that the only super power in the world, with the best command power, was denied the outcomes it desired.[25]

The Context of Globalization

Soft power has become extremely important because of globalization and the spread of the applications of information technology, especially the World Wide Web which has democratized information and knowledge. This has put power in the hands of individuals and has helped to form interest groups and communities cutting across state boundaries creating virtual communities with multiple identities.

Friedman argues that there have been three great eras of globalization. The first from 1492 when Columbus set sail opening trade between the Old World and the New World, until around 1800. It shrank the world from large to medium. Globalization was about countries and muscle. The driving force was, "brawn how much muscle, how much horse power, wind power or later, steam power your country had and how creatively you could deploy it." [26]

The second era of globalization lasted roughly from 1800 to 2000, interrupted by the Great Depression and World Wars I and II. This shrank the world from medium to small. The key agent of change in this era, the dynamic force driving global integration, was multinational companies. The multinationals went global for markets and labour, spearheaded first by the expansion of Dutch and English joint-stock companies and then the Industrial Revolution. In the first half of this era, the impetus was given by falling transportation costs, thanks to the steam engine and the railroad; and in the second half, by falling telecommunication costs because of the development of technology. The global economy matured because there was enough movement of goods and information from continent to continent to create a global market, and global arbitrage in products and labour.[27]

Around 2000, the third phase of globalization began. With it, the world shrank further from small to tiny and simultaneously flattened the playing field. What gives this phase of globalization its unique character is the new found power for individuals to collaborate and compete globally. The new information technology has made us all next-door neighbours. It is now for individuals to ask themselves where they fit into the global competition and opportunities of the day and they can, on their own, collaborate with each other globally. The individual empowerment is the most important new feature of globalization but companies, small and big, have also got newly empowered in this era.[28]

Further, the last century has seen large-scale migration for various reasons: displacement due to famines; droughts and other natural disasters; indentured labour; and movement of skilled human resource among others. India itself has seen at least three waves of migration because of indenture; skilled and semi-skilled workers to the Gulf region; and professionals and their families in search of better opportunities. In the last group there are many who have gone to developed countries such as the UK and the USA as students and have just stayed on there. When there is a critical mass of community in a nation-state its economic and political clout cannot be ignored. It may create conflict or it may make that nation-state sensitive to the concerns of that community both within that country and to issues pertaining to its home state. The home state also often leverages its diasporic community and those sympathetic to it, to voice its point of view in the international arena. Conversely, there is hardly any issue which does not have international ramifications, as has been experienced by India, whether it is pertaining to the Punjab or to Indo-US nuclear agreement. Thus, a new meaning has emerged of the idea of the geographical reach of a country as diasporic communities have spread across the world.

Hence, communities have been created that cut across national boundaries and exert pan global influences on their respective governments with regard to their political and other policies and decision-making. The world, in a globalized scenario, is being organized vertically by nation-states and regions but horizontally by an overlapping, permeable, multiple system of interaction. This creates communities not of place but of interests based on shared opinions and beliefs, ethnicities, religions, and even cuisines, consumption of medicines, lifestyles, fashion, music, and others. Societies have become multi-cultural, multi-ethnic, multi-lingual, multi-religious and often multi-citizen. National boundaries have been rendered porous because within the boundaries of a state, there are groups of people with multiple allegiances. The one single phenomenon that has exacerbated connectivity of people has been the internet, which has made it possible for people to communicate instantly, form virtual communities, access information at the touch of a button that would have taken months of determined hard work earlier, propagate ideas through mass e-mails and e-groups and develop skills available in different parts of the world without leaving the comforts of home.

Indian Context

India has always had close contacts with other nations, cultures, and civilizations of the world. The power of ideas is not unknown to it. According to Utpal Bannerji, in ancient times, the dialogues between nations was carried on through trade routes, leading to cross-fertilization of religious and philosophical thoughts, as well as the spreading of literary ideas, artistic styles and expressions. Indian ideas carried through its culture have left indelible footprints in different countries of South East Asia, Central Asia, and the Far East. Traders, travellers, priests, monks, scholars, sculptors, musicians, artists, and others have left Indian shores taking with them ideas and skills whose cross-fertilization with other cultures has been universally enriching.[29]

The Indus Valley civilization had its contacts with Central Asia, and in the Vedic period (1200 B.C.-600 B.C.) the Indian,

Iranian, and Central Asian civilization interacted through warriors, priests, and common people along with craftsmen such as metal workers, weavers, reed workers, and potters. According to Herodotus, in around 484 B.C., Indians were part of the Persian army. Taxila and Nalanda were important centres where all learning met and scholars came to them from several countries. Prince Mahendra and Princess Sanghamitra were sent as royal envoys with messages of the Buddha to Sri Lanka. The Silk Route connected China to the western world and brought many nationalities to Central Asia followed by the introduction of Buddhism there. It is believed that Central Asia played a unique role in disseminating Buddhism to China, Korea and Japan. The visits of Fa-Hein (fifth century), Huan-tsang, and Yi Jing (seventh century) are well known. Buddhism travelled to Korea from China and into Japan. Dharamabodhi and Barramon Sozzo were the cultural emissaries who went to Japan from Korea and made significant contributions to the traditions of Buddhist learning in Japan. It is believed that the *Panchtantra, Katha Saritsagar*, and *Jataka* tales, translated into Chinese reached Japan and became part of its folklore. Even today there is a large number of Sanskrit students in Japan.[30]

Cultural links between Cambodia and India began in the early Christian era (ninth to twelfth centuries) and it saw the development of Cambodian art in such monuments as Angkor Wat alongside the concept of Meru as Lord Shiva. The architecture from eastern India reached its artistic culmination at Borobuddur in Indonesia. The impact was that such cultural interaction became evident at various levels and provides a lesson to contemporary diplomacy.[31]

Political diplomacy played a very small role in these times. The chronicles of China, Korea, and Japan contain the timeless history of ancient India. It was the tradition of writing in China, Korea, and Japan that kept many written texts in Sanskrit intact as India had the tradition of oral history. The exchange of literature among countries helped enormously in enriching respective languages. The gains of cultural exchanges could be seen in architecture, painting, music, and dance and also in the penetration of the Indian martial arts into Chinese and Japanese traditions. In philosophy and scholarship also, the exchange was significant. The medieval period saw an influx of influences from Persia. Sufism and Islamic architecture stand testimony to the power of cultural exchange. India had a lot to offer in the fields of Mathematics, Philosophy, Astronomy, Medicine, and Sanskrit.[32] The conqueror and the conquered were profoundly influenced by each other.

Thus, India understood the power of ideas well. Many of these orientations found their way in certain formulations of India's foreign policy in post-independent India because any country has to function according to its cultural ethos and societal evolution. The foundations of India's foreign policy, obviously embodying its aspirations, were laid during the freedom movement itself. Nehru, its chief architect, suggested that while India may be a poor country it was also a great country that had a pivotal role to play in world affairs.

Factors Shaping India's Foreign Policy

Several factors were instrumental in shaping India's foreign policy: [33]

1. The struggle against imperialism and colonialism.
2. Viewing the world through the prism of the political, economic, and ideological contradictions and economic inequalities that had resulted in the two world wars.
3. The feeling that these contradictions and inequalities could not prevent tendencies of competition, conflict, and violence that affected the entire international community.

4. The unique nature of India's non-violent struggle for freedom as contrasted with other similar movements along with their resisting aggression and domination, led to the realization that each people and each society have their own aspirations, define the terms of reference for their respective struggles, and fashion their own methods to meet their objectives. There could be no imposed or uniform formula to manage the diversities of a complex world.

5. Consequently there was the conviction that international harmony, peace and stability could be achieved only by reasoning together, a commitment to cooperation rather than confrontation and an attitude that differences and diversities need not automatically translate into adversarial stances between states and societies.

6. If India was to contribute to the peace, stability, and well-being of the international community, it had to be responsive to the profound aspirations of common people. The process could no longer remain an esoteric exercise in structuring politico-military balances and furthering expansionist or acquisitive objectives of more powerful countries against the weaker ones. Therefore external relations had to be democratized. They had to become a participatory phenomenon in which public opinion played a vital role.

A country seeks to achieve its foreign policy objectives through diplomacy, which has a three-pronged approach: tacit acceptance of another country's position; understanding of its point of view and putting forth its own perspective and position; and carrying on a dialogue to make one's own position and approach acceptable. This dialogue in India was carried on since ancient times and India performed its role well. However, historical reasons interrupted the dialogue. After independence India, although bearing the scars of colonization and impoverishment, once again sought to resume it in an effort to find its own position in the world. Gradually, India's size, population, democratic institutions, development in economy, advances in science and technology, nuclear capability, and achievements in information technology, all gave it the potential to acquire a global status.

As Amit Gupta has pointed out, India by and large accepts the structure and order of the international system and only wants to improve its own power potential and status within it. India wants world peace and freedom as that is critical to its internal development and national security objectives. India naturally wants to have a say in world affairs.[34] So, while it has not signed the Nuclear Non-proliferation Treaty, its respect for international peace is evident from its refusal to assist in the proliferation of nuclear weaponry or its associated delivery systems. That is why it has consistently supported the United Nations and participated in over fifty peacekeeping operations including those in Korea, Egypt, and Congo in the earlier years and in Somalia, Angola, and Rwanda in recent years. One of India's long-term objectives is to become a permanent member of the United Nations Security Council.

India plays an important role in its own region as in the SAARC to strengthen regional cooperation. For example, with India's full support, SAARC has taken steps to accelerate economic cooperation. The South Asian Preferential Trade Agreement became operational in December 1995. In 1997, the 9th SAARC summit in Male when it was chaired by India, took a historical decision to strive for a South Asian Free Trade agreement (SAFTA) latest by 2001 A.D. The Indian Ocean Rim Association for Regional Cooperation also emerged in March 1997 as an important instrument of cooperation in the larger region with the active support of India. India has been following a 'Look East' policy as part of which it has been admitted as a full dialogue partner of ASEAN and a member of the ASEAN Regional Forum in 1996.[35]

India seeks decision-making roles as in being a pioneering member of the Law of the Seas Treaty and joining the Antarctic Club. Further, it wants to have enough economic power and adequate military might, while not inordinately squandering its resources on military expenditure, for other nations of the world to become sensitive to its point of view and factor it in during decision-making. Also, India seeks to provide intellectual leadership in the world and wishes to use multilateral agencies to develop itself economically. The combination of the two makes cooperation among nations easier to achieve in the long run. It also helps in projecting a favourable image of the nation. The Dutch international relations scholar, Peter van Ham, cited by Amit Gupta, has written about the rise of the "Brand State". A brand, according to him, "...is best described as a customer's idea of a product; the 'brand state' comprises the outside world's ideas about a particular country."[36] As van Ham further argues, "In today's world of information overload, strong brands are important in attracting foreign direct investment, recruiting the best and the brightest, and wielding political influence".[37]

Gupta shows how "India's global brand image has moved from a poor impoverished nation combined with outdated socialist ideas and a Victorian bureaucracy, to one of a tech-savvy, globalized, twenty-first century intellectual power."[38] India today is internationally known as the land of Bangalore, IITs, Infosys, Jet Airways, and outsourcing. This brand image is one that is best further developed and strengthened by soft power. In fact, one may argue that it is the new Indian brand image that further strengthens its soft power. Therefore, it is important for India to consciously develop policies through which it can use its soft power as a complement to its military and economic capability to develop the kind of external linkages it needs to help create stability in Asia, and facilitate its efforts to enter into cooperative economic and political arrangements in the world.

As Varun Sahni points out, at least three questions need to be answered:[39]

1. What power resources would India have at its command in the years to come?
2. Where would India be placed in the comity of nations?
3. How would India best use its power resources to carve out an appropriate niche for itself?

India cannot match the military might of developed nations and in any case, it evokes negative reactions and responses by causing fear, apprehension and resentment. A positive engagement is more desirable which also reduces the need to project military power. Economics and politics are important but other factors have come to the fore whose significance cannot be missed and which provide fertile fields for positive interaction. Cooperation and harmony are possible through educational and cultural linkages. They lead to benefits in strategic spheres also. These are 'soft' options but can be used effectively because instead of forcing people into certain positions, it is always better to hold hands and move in the same direction as far as possible. Further, soft options have the co-optive power that hard coercive options lack and are therefore, more enduring.

Cultural and educational diplomacy has received some attention in India through the Indian Council of Cultural Research (ICCR) and its programmes and through other educational exchanges but it has not been foregrounded to any large degree. Obviously there was some understanding of it immediately after India's independence which is obvious from India's efforts to provide educational support to the newly independent countries of Africa by sending teachers and giving scholarships to students to study in India. Many African students who studied in India came to occupy very important positions in their respective countries on their return. As part of colonial administration, Indians supplied teachers to many developing countries such as Burma or Myanmar, Fiji, and in East Africa to Uganda, Kenya, and Tanzania. Hence, Indians already had a well-recognized base but it was not built upon to the extent that it could have been. Then India's over 20 million strong diaspora is also its strength. Moreover, many students who come to India from Fiji, Malaysia, Mauritius, Sri Lanka and some countries of Africa and the Caribbeans for education belong to the Indian diaspora. They have strong emotional attachment to India and can be important goodwill ambassadors for it. In this educational institutions have to play a vital role but for them to do so effectively, the university system has to be sensitized.

Even cultural diplomacy cannot be effective without educational institutions and organizations being a part of the delivery system. This has been experienced. India has, for example, spent huge sums of money on organizing Festivals of India in different parts of the world but these have made a limited impact or they have reinforced the "exotic India" image because there has been little or no backing with education programme to create a greater in-depth understanding of the country and its people.

2

Education as an Instrument of Policy: America and India

The Ground Prepared

The end of World War II brought dramatic political, economic, and cultural changes in the world that empowered individuals and communities. But it took almost half a century for these changes to play out. The world went from the preeminence of the nation state to the foregrounding of the individual together with the formation of societies and communities that challenged the control of the nation state on the lives of individuals. In the West, political, economic, and cultural nationalism became discredited. On the other hand, in the developing world, nationalism in all its forms spread and intensified. In many developing countries, governments resorted to a multitude of controls, regulations and promotional policies that supported state-managed industrialization and restricted international trade and investment. In addition, a large portion of the world parted company with the open societies of the West and preferred Soviet style trade and investment policies. Centrally planned economies were installed in the Soviet sphere, on the Chinese mainland and elsewhere. Political pluralism was systematically eliminated in these countries. And, cultural imports were controlled and held to a minimum, while cultural exports were harnessed to expansionist political aims.

The post-World War II period also saw the emergence of the Cold War. This was a situation in which the United States and the erstwhile Soviet Union got locked in a fierce military competition pumping huge amounts of their GDPs into building, developing, and acquiring arms and arsenals. However, as the Cuban and the Vietnamese situation showed, the arms race did not lead to any significant results as both matched each other equally well.

Notwithstanding these factors, the United States was able to use its post-war industrial pre-eminence and influence to construct, with the support of the International Monetary Fund and the World Bank, a world economy with generally diminishing trade and investment barriers and open markets. Although the process of trade liberalization launched by the industrially advanced countries was long, often laborious, and fraught with contradictions, it nonetheless continued through the eight consecutive rounds of negotiations that composed the General Agreement on Tariffs and Trade (GATT) and that culminated in establishing the World Trade Organization (WTO). Exchange of goods and increasingly services skyrocketed, creating previously unknown levels of wealth and prosperity for many.

Alongside the institutional framework provided first by GATT and then by WTO, regional arrangements such as those that led to the European Union and the Southern Cone Common Market (Mercosur) in Latin America, were harbingers of the development of a global economy. By the 1980s, even the developing countries were turning to the kind of market-based policies that the advanced nations had been espousing. The collapse of communism after 1989 further extended the reach of this system to the countries of Central and Eastern Europe. A decade or so earlier, a shift in Chinese economic policy gradually opened a large portion of Asia to growing participation in world markets.[40]

In economic terms, the huge increase in the volume of trade went hand-in-hand with major changes in the organization of economic production. With barriers to trade effectively dismantled and technological changes dramatically facilitating transport and communications, companies could locate each stage of production in areas where factor costs were cheapest, allowing them to optimize sales of finished goods in the most lucrative markets. This expansion of trade, together with the geographical integration of production, came to be a significant piece of what came to be known as 'globalization'.

As Margaret Wyszomirski points out globalization is a "process in the works."[41] Economically, globalization is a process by which business expands into markets around the world because of the increasing integration of world markets and the different stages of production being located to areas with the most obvious competitive advantage. There is also the increasing interdependence of business and financial systems. Technologically, the internationalization of communications, media, and information delivery and distribution systems both support and drive the emerging global economy. Multinational and transnational communication and media corporations use wireless, fibre optic and web-based technologies to manage and market their products globally. The Internet and associated activities have made information access easier and faster than ever before. Apart from economic ramifications, one important consequence has been greater and greater interaction and communication among people round the world as they work, trade and exchange ideas with each other.

Therefore, as technology keeps evolving at a rapid pace, globalization is clearly about more than mere commerce.[42] Thomas Friedman notes in *The Lexus and the Olive Tree* : "Globalization...is the overarching international system shaping the domestic politics and foreign relations of virtually every country...." It [43]

> involves the inexorable integration of markets, nation-states, and technologies to a degree never witnessed before–in a way that is enabling individuals, corporations and nation-states to reach around the world farther, faster, deeper, and cheaper than ever before, and in a way that is also producing a powerful backlash from those brutalized or left behind. We have gone from How big is your missile? to How fast is your modem? We have gone from a variety of economic ideologies to a choice between, free market vanilla and North Korea.[44]

Along with the changes in economy, changes in social values and attitudes also become evident because changes in economy are linked to other aspects of a society, like social and political structures, the organization of civil society, preferences and beliefs, patterns of consumption, and the repertory of cultural expression. Communication technologies have speeded up globalization affecting cultural differences. Treasured features of societies and their cultural expressions are undergoing profound changes. This has made a number of countries express concern that culture is becoming "too global," in the sense that it is becoming too homogenized. This really becomes a euphemism for the apprehension that popular American culture is overpowering other cultures. It raises the question on how does culture work as a soft power and what apprehensions does it arouse in the case of a country which is perceived as overwhelmingly powerful; militarily, economically and politically. It can be asked that if soft power is really as effective as it is claimed to be, why is America's position not better understood ? One obvious reason is the natural anxiety and insecurity against a country that has the potential to overwhelm. However, Thomas Friedman counters any scepticism by arguing that, "[T]hanks in large part to increasing globalization more than one quarter of humanity is now enjoying growth at rates at which their living standards will quadruple within a generation.... That is unprecedented in economic history". And whatever resentment may be claimed in America that growth has not happened in the United States, but this worldwide growth has also led to the lowest unemployment rate in America in nearly fifty years.[45]

The Use of Soft Power: USA

The end of the Cold War created a unipolar world. It made USA both a military and economic super power. Perceiving no threat to its preeminence in the world, America's investment in the sphere of education and culture declined. This proved to be to its detriment. The terrorist attacks of September 11, 2001, brought this realization tragically home and led to a reconsideration of the subject. There is once again a renewed awareness that culture can be brought to the service to impact the way Americans are viewed by people in other parts of the world and that these perceptions are important in spite of all the power and resources available.

Culture creates human bonds, just as cultural division can tear a society apart. Underlying cultural assumptions shape trade, commerce, and laws. Cultural strife can make all these institutions dysfunctional. Therefore, argues Feigenbaum, the configuration and production of culture is a legitimate concern of public policy as it comprises both public and private good.[46] Further, in a world where literally everyone has become everyone else's neighbour, it is absolutely essential to understand and respect each other's culture if there is to be cooperation, whether in trade and commerce or in solving global problems like degradation of environment, human rights, issues pertaining to women and children and others. The empowerment of the individual has shifted the focus from mere brute strength and markets to individual well-being and creation of conditions in the collective to ensure it.

Even economically, as Hawey B. Feigenbaum observes in the American context, education and spread of knowledge are required to increase competitiveness because national and global economies are increasingly based on information and its exchange.[46] To facilitate this, the US government has encouraged exchange programmes that allow people from different countries and cultures to get to know and understand each other. In US public diplomacy has enlisted the aid of culture to hopefully try and create an understanding about America's perspective in a persuasive way to hopefully receptive publics in other nations. Such an environment is absolutely essential to economic activity that requires different kinds of skills from those required for mass production. From modest repetitive skills, the shift has been to knowledge-based skills and knowledge is acquired through institutions that are shaped by culture. For this the education system and especially universities are vital.

Feigenbaum goes on to illustrate how public funding has been very effective in promoting higher education and research. Connecting with the world expands the knowledge base of educational institutions and improves the quality of research.[47] This is often accomplished through public–private partnerships. Shalini Venturelli of the American University and other thoughtful analysts have argued that the cultural wealth of a nation is the key to the new economy.[48] Her basic argument is that cultural wealth can no longer be regarded as something fixed which is inherited and mass distributed. It has to be tested by its capacity to produce and generate ideas through knowledge, energy, and dynamism. Thus the pursuit of knowledge and the encouragement of creativity are related but not identical. Nor is its cultivation limited to higher education. Venturelli's argument is that this goal has to pervade the entire education system at all levels. Basic literary skills and sufficient learning enough to create a capacity to follow instructions on the assembly line in the workshop, or at the desktop terminals have become inadequate for the demands of a creative and innovative society. Therefore, what is needed is not just basic education, but advanced intellectual and creative skills that emphasize interdisciplinary and independent thinking and these have to be acquired at the earliest stages of the educational process that extend from preschool to higher education.[49]

Culture has been important to America's relations with the rest of world in a number of ways. It is increasingly so not only because trade in cultural goods and services has increased manifold but also because culture can be both a source of cooperation and conflict. William Glade has traced the growth and impact of two sets of policies, educational exchange and cultural diplomacy in the American context.[50] Of these, trans-border educational interactions date back to the late 1700s when the newly established learned societies were organized and their members started communicating with members of similar organizations in Europe and Latin America. Benjamin Franklin, he points out, was the first American to be selected for membership in the Spanish Academy of History, and the American Philosophical Society established in 1743 was the first learned society to elect Europeans and Spanish Americans as corresponding members. Before the mid-1800s, many Americans went out of the country to study the arts and humanities. At the same time, American missionaries went to Asia and the Middle East which resulted in the earliest foreign students coming to the USA. By 1900, American universities and museums were sponsoring overseas expeditions, some to the Mediterranean area and others to Latin America, where there was already a presence of American artists and writers. After World War I, bilateral and multilateral assistance programmes in America poured resources into institution building in education. This expanded opportunities for students and established scholars to study, research and work in America.

The most important advance in educational exchange took place after World War II through the prestigious programmes initiated by Senator J. William Fulbright. It paved the way for participation in exchange programmes in the arts, predominantly in the social sciences and humanities, and was strengthened by the government's concurrent promotion of American Studies abroad. Other exchange programmes were also initiated. Glade shows how these programme not only contribute to a genuine exchange of ideas, scholarship, and skill among participating countries, but are also economically beneficial.[51] Richard J. Arndt, long time diplomat and former president of the Fulbright Association, has also said that although the dividends for the American society and economy are not always obvious, since the investment in foreign relations does not become evident for a decade or two but the benefits are certainly there :

> Students return to their countries and begin almost immediately to shape attitudes, create new demands, launch new needs and open new markets for the US experience and products.... Cultural exchanges are certainly not designed to boost the economy, but economic advantages like propaganda-flow as a natural by product.[52]

The US government's strategy is usually to provide the seed money and then to encourage the private sector to take over. That is why since the beginning of the twentieth century the biggest players in this area have been large foundations, non-profit organizations, and academic institutions. Glade notes:

> Not long into the twentieth century, missionary founders were joined (then overshadowed) by secular foundations in promoting educational development and exchanges. The first, the Rockefeller Foundation, was only a year old when in 1914 it set up the China Medical Board to introduce Western medicine.[53]

Thus, exchanges of all kinds were set up by foundations that included education, research and the arts. American culture became more dynamic because of the constant exchange of ideas, scholarship and work, coupled with the flow of immigrants who brought with them their own knowledge base, hard work, value system, and determination to succeed. However, according to Glade, the non-governmental educational exchanges were the most important cultural link between the USA and the rest of the world until just before World War II. Thus learned societies and institutions related to higher education laid the foundation for long-term international cultural relations.[54] Maturing in the 1920s, some of the prominent institutions and organizations were the Institute for International Education, the American Library Association, the American Council of Learned Societies, and the American branch of the Committee on Intellectual Cooperation of the League of Nations. Other initiatives sprang, directly or indirectly, from such gatherings like the 1936 Inter-American Conference for the Maintenance of Peace. Such initiatives led the State Department to establish in 1938 its first Division of Cultural Relations making cultural diplomacy explicit public policy.

As World War II engulfed more and more countries, US national security interests seemed to require paradoxically enough, that more rather than less overt attention needed to be paid to cultural diplomacy. This paved the way for post-war uses of cultural diplomacy to support the spread of Western democratic ideas. Glade states:

> A course-altering decision was taken in 1938 when the Division of Cultural Relations was set up in the Department of State. Thus began the new function of cultural diplomacy, with which education exchanges were joined.
>
> A secular replay of the old missionary impulse, cultural diplomacy was conceived as persuasively telling the story of America's cultural accomplishments, and social, political, and economic procedures, to the world—and, secondarily, promoting greater knowledge of foreign cultures.[55]

But as Kevin Mulcahy warns:

> [E]xchanges must be distinguished from propaganda. Both are legitimate activities of governments as they seek to project their interests abroad. Propaganda has an admittedly negative connotation, but as used here simply refers to the range of information and psychological activities (such as films, news stories and broadcasts) that seek to explain to other people what American foreign policy is about. Such informational diplomacy has an explicit, immediate political content; cultural diplomacy does not: its methods are

> indirect and its goals are long-range. Informational diplomacy uses the techniques of public relations (and sometimes psychological warfare), while cultural diplomacy is rooted in education and example. In sum, cultural diplomacy rests on the premise that allowing American cultural activities and leaders to speak for themselves abroad is the best advertising for the virtues of a free society. That the goal is political—projecting a favourable image of American society abroad—must be appreciated; but, that the methods of cultural diplomacy—the free exchange of ideas, events, and peoples—are [in some sense] non-political has been less well-understood and perhaps even less appreciated.[56]

However as the NAFSA (Association of Foreign Education Providers) document on why America needs a policy for international education points out, after the end of the Cold War, the emphasis on international education in America seems to have lessened.[57] Talking of the need for an international education policy in America, NAFSA emphasizes its importance for at least two reasons. First, in the current globalized scenario, the USA cannot expect to retain its competitive edge if its workforce lacks strong international and cross-cultural knowledge and skills. Second, the tragic event of September 11, 2001 is a forceful reminder that the Cold War may have ended but it is still a dangerous world and it is necessary to understand it. To do so, skill in the languages of the world is required to promote better understanding of the USA by the world's citizens. NAFSA and the Alliance for International Educational and Cultural Exchange, in 1999, were the first to call for an international education policy. Since then, others have added their voices. According to a December 2005 national poll commissioned by NAFSA, 90 per cent of Americans believed that is was necessary to prepare future generations for a global society. It has been felt that the need is critical because globalization was obliterating the distinction between foreign and domestic concerns. Today, most domestic problems were also international problems. Further global economic and technology revolutions were reshaping business, work, and life where constant interaction with others was needed. Different kinds of knowledge and skills were required to take the opportunities offered in a globalized world where information and communication were at the touch of a button.

Very interestingly, the NAFSA document points out that internationalized education is important because USA not only imparts scientific and technological knowledge to others but is itself dependent on international scientific and technological talent. This is making educational exchange relationships more complex, because the USA now not only has an interest in educating international students and returning them to contribute to the leadership and development of their home countries, but it also needs to hire them to fill positions in its high-technology industries and research establishments.

Further, international education is more important for US international leadership and security than ever before according to NAFSA because alliances and international relationships matter. Exchange relationships sustain political relationships; if one atrophies, sooner or later the other will too. Having fewer future world leaders study in the United States must necessarily result in a loss of US international influence down the road.

Impact of USA on Indian Education

The power of education to mould the body, heart, mind, and intellect is often forgotten in India. Education penetrates all aspects of the psyche and shapes the personality thereby becoming a strong motivating force in a person's actions. We often tend to forget the power of educational influences but it is evident in the very foundations of higher education in India; in its institutions and structures as they are largely derived from the British model. The influence of British education is felt not only in the basic structure of Indian higher education but also in the range of the most elite institutions in India today.

In the post-independence era, USA replaced UK in its impact on Indian education. The Indian Institutes of Technology (the IITs) were consciously patterned after MIT in the USA and received substantial overseas help right from the outset. With support from four donor nations, the five IITs benefited from guest faculty from outside India; from the ability to send Indian faculty abroad for training; and from contributions of modern laboratory equipment and facilities. The spin-off effects of that collaboration are evident to all today. If India is considered a leader in Information Technology, the movement has been driven largely by IIT graduates in the Silicon Valley in California, USA. It has also led to Bangalore becoming the Silicon Valley of Asia. Successful IITians want to help more in this field, as the relationship is mutually beneficial. It has had a great effect on India's standing in the world and has contributed greatly to changing India's image from an underdeveloped country to a knowledge-based society. Similarly, international links were also established by the Indian Institutes of Management (IIMs). Indira Gandhi National Open University (IGNOU) and other state-sponsored Open Universities drew heavily from the UK experience with distance education and the Open University concept.

Why did so many Indian professionals make the USA their country of adoption? One important reason perhaps is that the USA became one of the most important countries for higher education replacing Great Britain, at least for Indians.

Education for the Indian middle class was through English and therefore language, which could have been a major hurdle, proved no barrier. Thousands of Asians studied in the USA after 1960. Before the 1965 amendments, about 50,000 foreign students attended American universities. By 1981 the figure had reached approximately 300,000, Asians, Indians accounting for nearly half of the total. Many stayed on and adjusted their resident status. In 1978, ten years after the 1965 Act came into full force, over 18,000 non-immigrant students became immigrants, of which two-thirds were Asians. A survey of National Science Foundation (NSF) of scientists and engineers immigrating to the USA in the first five years of the new immigration system that is from 1966-1970, of the new immigration system, revealed that 60 per cent had been in the US on a temporary basis some time before they had become immigrants and that a majority had actually lived there before they acquired a residential status.[58] Ten years later the NSF found that the number of foreigners earning Ph.Ds in Engineering, Physical Sciences, and Mathematics had increased from the late 1960s.[59] The Labour Department also reported that students who completed their education in the USA were more likely to stay on and work there.

Among the Asians, Indians trailed the Filipinos, Chinese, and Koreans in number because few had emigrated before 1950 and not many possessed the kinship network to take advantage of the 1965 law immediately. However, India increased its immigration substantially in the decade after 1965, the figure being over 115,000 in that ten-year span. In 1976, immigration from India crossed 17,000, went over 18,000 in 1977, and over 22,000 in 1980. Gradually India was becoming one of the largest source nations for skilled human resource for America.[60] The first Indian immigrants after 1965 were predominantly males who took jobs in American urban hospitals, universities, or businesses. Next to the Filipinos and Koreans, Indians made up the largest contingent of East Asian medical professionals, including nurses and physicians.

However, all Indian professionals were not physicians. They also included scientists and engineers. In 1978, the NSF reported that Asia accounted for slightly more than half of the immigrant scientists and engineers of that year. India had the largest number of any nation and accounted for one-third of the Asian total. These were mostly engineers.[61]

One of the reasons, perhaps, of why so many Indian professionals went to USA and why so many students regarded it as their educational Mecca could also be the extraordinary and extensive collaboration between India and the USA in spite of the fluctuating fortunes of political relationship between the two countries in the last fifty years. The American role in India's development began in 1951 with a total assistance of $12,138 million through September 1985. American assistance was used in various projects to increase India's self-sufficiency. Cooperation in the fields of Science and Technology encompassed core areas such as agriculture, fertilizer plants, forestry and also agriculture universities and raising educational institutions. Many of India's leading scientists today began work as young researchers in the Indo-USA research projects. Over the years, 3000 American technicians, agronomists, engineers and doctors came to India to help with food and agriculture projects and 6000 Indians went to the USA for training. [62]

Between 1952 and 1972, American universities entered into partnership agreements with Indian institutions to establish agricultural universities. The universities involved were those of Illinois, Kansas, Missouri, Ohio, Pennsylvania, and Tennessee and the agriculture universities that emerged were situated in the Punjab, Haryana, Uttar Pradesh, Orissa, Maharashtra, Andhra Pradesh, and Karnataka. During this period more than 300 American teachers gave over 700 teaching years worth of service and at least a thousand Indian faculty members and students trained in the USA.

Between 1954 and 1966 the universities of Illinois, Wisconsin, and Michigan provided visiting professors and equipment to IIT Kharagpur, Colleges of Engineering in Pune the Bengal Engineering College in Howrah, and the University College of Engineering in Roorkee. Through US-Aid, regional engineering colleges were established and over the years, hundreds of educators went for training to the USA. However, one of the most significant contributions was the setting up of IIT Kanpur in 1962. Prof. Dahl who had enlisted the support of America's top technical universities—Massachusetts Institute of Technology (MIT), California Institute of Technology, Ohio State University, Princeton University, University of California at Berkeley, University of Michigan and Perdue University, and who had donated more than 40,000 books and journals, led the first group of MIT professors to teach at Kanpur. By 1972, when the programme formally ended, the consortium of universities had taught 2000 teaching years, 50 faculty members had received advanced training in the USA, and the Institute had received laboratory equipment worth $8 million.

Then there were programmes of International Corps Research Institute for Semi-Arid Tropics (ICRISAT) and work done by the Ford Foundation, the Rockefeller Foundation, the Fulbright programmes, the American Studies Research Centre, and the American Institute of Indian Studies. Jointly they created a huge educational pool of scholars, scientists, and technicians in both countries who knew and understood each other. The underlying central belief was that over the longer term, active contacts between the professional elite of the two countries would be vital for the health of Indo-US friendship.[63]

That vision can now be seen as coming to fruition to the benefit of both the countries. About 1.5 million people of Indian origin live in the USA. The median income of the Indian American family is $60,000 as compared to the national median income of about $39,000. Over 5000 Indian Americans serve as faculty in universities across America. Over 300,000 Indian Americans work in the information technology field with an average income of $200,000 a year. In the Silicon Valley, Indians live in the Bay area and work in the high tech domain. They are about 200,000 Indians and they have formed an incredible network. They invest in one another's companies, sit on one another's boards and hire each other in key jobs. Collectively, they have created companies that account for $235 billion of the market value. Indian engineers have gone to the USA since the early 1970s, a large number of them being from the IITs. The rise of the IITians is a telling example of how global capitalism works today. The best companies draw on the best brains from around the world. By rising to the top of Corporate America, these IIT alumni lead all other Asians in their ability to reach the upper echelons of world class companies.

The IIT graduates, however, have also not forgotten their alma mater, which has given them such good education. A few years ago, thirteen CEOs who had all made their fortunes in Silicon Valley offered to raise $500 million dollars for the development of the IITs. Under certain conditions their contribution could go up to $1billion. Another group of Indian-born, US-based software engineers wanted to raise an equal amount to set up a series of world-class centres of higher learning in India. Even individual expatriate Indians are donating to high-tech causes. For example, Rekhi gave $5 million to IIT Mumbai in 1998 to establish a school of information technology to be named after him. Desh Deshmukh has pledged $100 million over the next twenty years to his alma mater, IIT Madras. In August 1999, N. R. Narayana Murthy head of the fund raising committee and the then Chair of Infosys Technologies Ltd. of Bangalore raised $1 million during a single lunch meeting in San Francisco. He himself gave an individual contribution of $2 million to the school for a new computer laboratory. There are many such examples.[64]

Not only have Indians distinguished themselves in different fields of science, technology, medicine, entrepreneurship, academics, computers, engineering, informatics, they are also gaining a political voice. They are seen as important fundraisers. They realize that it is not enough to just have money. Political voice is equally important. Many wealthy Indian Americans support political parties or candidates who are sympathetic to India. High-tech entrepreneur Vish Akella initiated a $400,000 fundraiser for the Democratic Party and Sabeer Bhatia of the Hotmail fame hosted a fundraiser for Gore that raised $600,000. An India Caucus has been formed to look after India's interests with American government and legislature. According to Dr. Kishan Aggarwal, the Association of American Physicians of Indian Origin (AAPI) has played a crucial role in Indo-American relationship.[65] The AAPI members maintain a legislative office in Washington to keep track of bills that will affect them professionally and also those that affect America's relationship with India. Once a year they organize "AAPI on the Hill", a full day's programme where invited Congressmen discuss immigration, discrimination, and other issues concerning Indian Americans. More and more Indian Americans are likely to get involved in the political process especially the second generation who will not be just fund raisers but participate more actively in the civic life and polity of the country as they are born and brought up in the US and regard themselves as primarily American.[66]

3

Educational and Cultural Diplomacy in India

Indian Council of Cultural Relations

Cultural diplomacy has received sporadic attention in India, but educational diplomacy has received hardly any attention. Although there is some writing on the subject, it has certainly not been foregrounded in foreign policy discussions. Whatever initiatives have been taken in this area have been by the Ministry of External Affairs but it does not seem to even impinge on the consciousness of either Ministry of Human Resource Development or of University Grants Commission or of the universities or of other decision making bodies in the field of higher education. Obviously there was some understanding of it immediately after India's independence as is evident from the setting up of Indian Council of Cultural Relations and the educational support programs for developing countries.

With the achievement of Independence in 1947, India was inevitably drawn into the mainstream of international activities. While internally the government and its leaders grappled with problems of economic, social and cultural development, India began to play a leading role abroad in the sphere of international peace and amity. The move to revive cultural ties with the world outside was in fact an integral part of the nationalist movement and the struggle for independence.

The Indian Council of Cultural Relations (ICCR) was formally set up in 1950 within the ambit of the Ministry of External Affairs. Its primary objective was to establish, revive and strengthen cultural relations and mutual understanding between India and other countries. Its foundation was laid by two leaders, Pandit Jawaharlal Nehru, the first Prime Minister of India who was his own External Affairs Minister and Maulana Abul Kalam Azad, the first Minister for Education. They fostered the idea of an autonomous council which would act as a cultural bridge of understanding between India and the rest of the world.

Maulana Azad in his inaugural address at the ICCR, New Delhi, on April 9, 1950, expressed his happiness that the setting up of the Council had been warmly welcomed by different foreign countries.[67] Egypt, Syria, Lebanon, Iraq, Iran, Afghanistan, Myanmar or Burma, and Sri Lanka or Ceylon had all expressed strong support for the proposal. Maulana Azad hoped that cultural relations with these countries would continually expand and that there would be full cooperation and interaction between universities and other cultural and learned societies of India and these countries. He then outlined some steps that would be taken which included among others facilities to scholars for the study of history and culture of these countries. To begin with, he presented his own library to the Council and the Ajit Ghosh collection containing many rare and valuable books on Indian art and architecture were bought. A reading room was set up where magazines, newspapers and journals of different countries together with publications of universities and cultural societies would be available. Other activities outlined were periodic meetings of specialists, exchange of professors and the study of various languages, especially those associated with ancient civilizations and cultures. In the first issue of *Indo-Asian Culture* published by the Council, Maulana Azad said:

> In the British period in particular, the eyes of Indians turned more towards the West. Political subjugation meant a large degree of intellectual domination. Nevertheless, with the first awakening of national consciousness, the Indian desire of rejuvenating old contacts with our old friends revived. Even before the British had left, the old relations were sought to be restored and Rabindranath Tagore went in the countries of South East Asia and the Far East as India's unofficial cultural ambassador. That the desire for friendship was mutual was evident from the love and affection with which all these countries received him and welcomed the message of India. India is now keen to revive her old friendly contacts with all countries of the world. In such a context is it surprising that she should be particularly anxious to be friends with those who are our neighbours to the east and the west?[68]

Jawaharlal Nehru in his inaugural address also emphasized the importance of cultural exchanges as an instrument of international understanding. He observed:

> A race or a group does not count for much unless it has roots in the past, which past, after all is the accumulation of generations of experience and some type of wisdom...

> on the other hand, one cannot live in the roots alone.
>
> The roots even wither unless they come out in the sun and the free air and then roots give you sustenance, also giving you all kinds of things and branching out and flowering. And then one might say that you have balance.[69]

However, Nehru was aware that while culture was an instrument of cooperation, it could also lead to conflict. "One thing that troubles me in this", he said

> was that often enough people, who understand each other more and more, begin to quarrel more and more.
>
> Therefore it becomes essential that we must try to understand each other in the right way. The right way is important. The right approach, the friendly approach, the friendly approach is important because a friendly approach brings a friendly response.
>
> So if we approach our fellow human beings or other countries in the right way, not in any sense of surrendering anything that we consider of essential value to truth or to our own genius, but nevertheless in a friendly way, with our minds and hearts open and prepared to accept whatever good comes to them, then that will lead, not only to understanding, but the right type of understanding...[70]

Keeping in view this vision, the aims of ICCR were enunciated as follows:[71]

(i) To participate in the formulation and implementation of policies and programmes relating to India's external cultural relations;

(ii) To foster and strengthen cultural relations and mutual understanding between India and other countries;

(iii) To establish and develop relations with national and international organization in the field of culture.

To attain these objectives, ICCR has put into place major academic and educational programmes like scholarship schemes for overseas students the emphasis being on developing countries; establishing and maintaining chairs and professorships for Indian studies abroad; presentation of books, audio-visual material, art objects and musical instruments; annual organization of the Maulana Azad Memorial lecture and Maulana Azad essay competition; and organization of other programmes on behalf of the Ministry of External Affairs. Beside these, it has several publications, organizes and participates in international seminars and symposia, and does other such activities. That the institution has so many academic-related activities indicates an awareness about education as the medium through which culture and values can be disseminated. The belief is that overseas students help in building bridges of understanding and developing a better appreciation of India. They have the enormous potential of spreading goodwill for India in their respective countries. Hence the idea is to make the Indian experience for foreign students as attractive as possible by facilitating their passage into academic institutions, maintaining contact with them, coordinating with foreign students' advisers in the universities, helping the students with accommodation and arranging language classes and orientation programmes where required.

This vision, that it is important to build understanding among people and thereby among nations, has been manifested not only in ICCR but in several other programmes of the Ministry of External Affairs. For example, the Government of India provides fifty scholarships each year to deserving Bhutanese students in different professional streams like Medicine, Engineering, Law, Nursing, Agriculture, Dentistry and others. In addition, Ambassador's scholarships are awarded to meritorious and deserving Bhutanese students after they have been admitted to various schools and colleges in India. Further there is the Technical Cooperation Scheme of the Colombo Plan, through which the Government of India provides comprehensive and integrated training to foreign participants to upgrade their administrative and technical skills. Under this scheme, fifty short, medium and long-term training slots are provided to the Bhutanese every year. There are other programmes of the Government of India like the SAARC scholarship scheme and a six-week professional course for Foreign Diplomats, the latter being run three or four times a year by the Foreign Service Institute of the Ministry of External Affairs.

ITEC Programme

However, the most important is the Indian Technical and Economic Cooperation or the ITEC programme run by the Ministry of External Affairs.[72] It was launched by a decision of the Indian Cabinet on September 15, 1964 as a bilateral programme of assistance. Its chief architect was Jawaharlal Nehru, who was also the External Affairs Minister at that time. Even before independence, India had attached great importance to cooperation between developing countries and had been an active participant in UN Commonwealth multilateral aid programmes and had also been giving aid to neighbours like Nepal and Bhutan, on a bilateral basis. However, the ITEC programme was envisaged as a major bilateral programme of economic assistance to other developing countries. Through it and its corollary Special Commonwealth Assistance for Africa Programme (SCAAP), 156 countries in Asia, East and Central Europe (including Russia), Central Asia, Africa, Latin America and the Pacific are invited to share in the Indian developmental experience garnered since independence.

ITEC envisages cooperation and partnership for mutual benefit. It is response-oriented and it addresses the needs of developing countries. It embodies the spirit of South/South Cooperation. While India in the early 1960s could not give grants-in-aid to match those of developed countries, its strength lay in its skills of human resource and technology that were more appropriate for developing countries than those of developed countries. The programme has six components: training in India of nominees of ITEC partner countries, both civilian and military; projects and project-related activities such as feasibility studies and consultancy services; deputation of Indian experts abroad; study tours; Aid for Disaster Relief (ADR); and gifting or donation of equipment at the request of ITEC partner countries. Although ITEC is essentially bilateral, occasionally the resources have been used for financing Trilateral and Regional Programmes, for example, under the Economic Commission for Africa (UNECA), United Nations Industrial Development Organization (UNIDO) and Group of 77. The Afro Asian Rural Development Organization (AARDO) and G-15 are also helped by ITEC with training and project support. Also special and customized programmes have been designed for regional and multilateral groupings such as the Association of Southeast Asian Nations (ASEAN), Bay of Bengal Initiative for Multi Sectoral Technical and Economic Cooperation (BIMSTEC), the African Union (AU), Caribbean Community and Common Market (CARICOM), the Commonwealth and the World Trade Organization (WTO).

India spends about Rs. 50 crores annually on ITEC activities, and has provided over US $ 2.5 billion worth of technical assistance to developing countries, including its neighbour countries since 1964. Over 45,000 people have participated in ITEC programmes attending courses in various disciplines. Many of them work in important positions in their respective countries.

In addition to the training courses, ITEC takes its participants to 'Outstation Study Tours' to introduce them to India, its democratic system, culture and historical heritage. It brings home India as a vibrant democracy with a strong pluralistic flavour which provides a model of development to many developing countries. The training courses cover a wide variety of subjects such as Information Technology (IT); Parliamentary Studies; Mass Communication; English Language Courses; Rural Development; Bank Management; Educational Planning and Administration; Entrepreneurship Development; Secretariat Training and Management; Food Technology; Tool Design; Manpower Research; Statistical Education; Non-Conventional Energy Resources; Entrepreneurship and Small Business Development; Water Resources and others. For example, for the year 2006-07, thirty-nine institutions were identified for civilian training and they were empanelled to conduct 222 courses. Further, study tours in India are undertaken at the specific request of ITEC beneficiary countries. Specific areas of interest are also identified for two or three-week programmes during which delegates visit important institutions and training centres in different parts of India.

An important element of ITEC is promotion of India's technology in various areas like agriculture, machinery, textiles, pharmaceutical and information technology. This increases diplomatic and strategic space for India as it builds bonds of friendship and shared values through training in defence, democratic institutions, modern science and technology. It has created considerable goodwill for India and has helped to enhance its image as a country with technological skills and capabilities which it is willing to share with other developing countries.

Military Training in all the three wings of the Defence Services is provided to a select number of countries in prestigious institutions such as the National Defence College, New Delhi and National Defence Services Staff College, Wellington. The training covers a number of fields and on an average around 350 defence personnel attend courses every year including from advanced countries.

Then there are the project assistance programmes which show India's technological and human resource capacities. One major focus of project assistance is agriculture. Other areas are vocational training in small-scale industries and entrepreneurship Information Technology, biotechnology and law. Together with this, India also provides feasibility studies and consultancy services at the request of ITEC partner countries. Further, public sector undertakings bid for developmental projects in developing countries. Indian experts are deputed to countries on request to assist in developmental activities. They study the problems and suggest solutions without disturbing the local socio-economic and cultural environment. India's experience in the fields of small-and medium-scale industries, agriculture and financial management are particularly relevant to developing countries. In addition, India provides aid for disaster relief like supply of medicines and food stuffs in times of need.

The ITEC programme demonstrates India's role and contribution in South-South cooperation. The Ministry of External Affairs acknowledges the contributions of the programmes towards

- capacity-building and human resource development in many parts of the world

> where they are most needed. India is seen as a provider of technical know-how and expertise, extending training, consultancy services, and conducting surveys and feasibility reports. Besides, a strong culture of understanding, camaraderie and friendship and networking is a by-product of the programme. Over the years the technical assistance work has become one of the mainstream activities of the Ministry of External Affairs as well as a major instrument of India's foreign policy and it has generated substantive dividends and immense goodwill over the last four decades.[73]

International Environment

While there is no thought of higher education as an instrument of India's external relations in other educational agencies apart from the Ministry of External Affairs, they have begun to discuss the issue of internationalization of higher education. This has been largely triggered by the impact of globalization, the exodus of Indian students to foreign universities in India, the setting up of centres by foreign universities in India and their drive to recruit Indian students, the availability of degrees online through the Internet and other such factors. Internationally, too, education has been a subject of much debate and discussion in the last ten years. October 1998, for instance, was a very significant year for the world of higher education as representatives of 128 nations responsible for education, including higher education, met for the first time in Paris under the auspices of UNESCO to discuss issues of common concern and to agree on the general direction that higher education must take in the present century. The Conference was unanimously of the view that a renewal of higher education was essential for the whole society to face the challenges of the twenty-first century. These included intellectual independence of individual creation and advancement of knowledge; and education and training to shape responsible enlightened citizens and qualified specialists, without whom no nation could progress economically, socially, culturally or politically. The Declaration of the World Conference emphasized that since society was increasingly knowledge-based, higher education and research had become essential components of cultural, socio-economic and environmentally sustainable development of individuals, communities and nations. The development of higher education, therefore, ranked as among the highest national priorities of nations throughout the world as without it, the required human resource could not be created.

In convening this conference, the UNESCO reaffirmed its strong commitment to fostering the development of higher education and research. One of the objectives was to generate a broad debate on it to complement the major conferences in the field of education that constituted landmarks in the process of its renewal. Some of these were the World Conference on Education for All (Jomtien, Thailand, 1990), the 45th session of the International Conference on Education on the Role of Teachers in a Changing World (Geneva, 1996) and the International Conference on Adult Education (Hamburg, 1997). In addition, the World Conference reiterated the recommendations relating to the opening up of higher education made by the International Commission on Education for the Twenty-First Century in Learning: The Treasure Within (1996).

The Conference was preceded by a widespread mobilization of partners, national policy makers, institutional leaders, professors, researchers, students, professional sectors and others. Regional Conferences were held in Havana in November 1996, Dakar in April 1997, Tokyo in July 1997, Palermo in September 1997, and Beirut in March 1998.

Findings, declarations and plans of action of these conferences provided inputs for the Paris Conference. These were complemented by studies and analyses undertaken by some fifty governmental and non-governmental organizations charged with preparing a series of thematic debates on important issues of higher education. Twelve debates were structured around three main domains. The first was on higher education and development considered as requirements for the world of work. Under this were to be considered higher education and sustainable human development contributing to national and regional development; and higher education staff development as a continuous process. The second domain was new trends and innovations in higher education that encompassed students' vision of higher education for a new society; the use of new information technologies; challenges and opportunities in research and the contribution of higher education to the education system as a whole. The third domain dealt with higher education and its relationship with culture and society. It had under its umbrella, women and higher education; promoting a culture of peace; mobilizing the power of culture; autonomy and social responsibility and higher education.

At the Conference itself the delegates dealt with issues pertaining to the changing missions of higher education in the twenty-first century. These included interaction of higher education with society; the impact of the change process on higher education together with diversification; increased flexibility of systems and promotion of lifelong learning; and access to higher education. All these factors provided elements that went into the Declaration and Framework for Action that the Conference adopted at the end as "World Declaration on Higher Education for the Twenty-First Century: Vision and Action" and "Framework for Priority Action for Change and Development of Higher Education". The Conference resolved that "beyond its traditional functions of teaching, training, research and study, all of which remain fundamental", higher education must "promote development of the whole person and train responsible, informed citizens, committed to working for a better society in the future". It has led to intense activity around the world as country after country has tried to assess the role of higher education in development and what needs to be further done.

The Task Force on Higher Education and Society was convened by the World Bank and UNESCO in the year 2000 to bring together some of the world's foremost education and development experts. Based on research, intensive discussion and hearings conducted over a two-year period, the Task Force concluded that without more and better education, developing countries would find it increasingly difficult to benefit from the global knowledge-based economy.

Internationalization of Higher Education in India

The Indian higher education system is now recognized as one of the better systems for producing a talented human workforce. Various agencies connected with education have begun to seriously look at the merits and demerits of internationalization of higher education in India. The National University of Education Planning and Administration (NUEPA) deliberated upon issues pertaining to globalization and the response to internationalization of education in a national conference held in New Delhi in August 2004. It felt that challenges of quality, modes of supply; access and equity in higher education; responses to General Agreement on Trade in Services (GATS) and WTO, matters pertaining to identity, culture and curriculum; and other concerns of the nations receiving foreign higher education need to be addressed.[74] On the one hand there was a recognition of the benefits that internationalization of education could bring but there were also serious apprehensions leading to ambivalence of attitude.

The Association of Indian Universities (AIU) too held roundtables on internationalization of higher education, the first at the University of Mysore in February 2001 and the second at Guru Nanak Dev University in Amritsar in February 2002.[75] Of course, neither the recommendations of the Mysore roundtable which are known as the "Mysore Statement" nor the subsequent recommendations at Amritsar viewed the internationalization of education as a soft power but they accepted that it was a fact of life in the new knowledge era and had to be done if India was to be counted as a knowledge society. There was a realization that internationalization would lead to an improvement in the quality of education, promote Indian culture abroad, generate goodwill and understanding; and yield financial benefits. It was recognized that partnership and networking were essential for enriching the teaching-learning process and for improved quality of research. Hence, it was necessary to act in earnest without further delay and so the government, academic institutions and Association of Indian Universities were all urged to take the necessary steps to promote Indian higher education internationally. To achieve this end several recommendations were made. The Amritsar recommendations built on the Mysore Statement and reinforced it.

Further, the University Grants Commission (UGC), in the Tenth Plan (2002-2007) made internationalization of higher education one of its thrust areas and projected a vision for promoting Indian Higher Education abroad as a response to the phenomenon of globalization. The Chairman UGC set up an Expert Committee to encourage the free flow of students from other nations to India and vice versa. Subsequently, a Standing Committee of UGC for the Promotion of Indian Higher Education Abroad (PIHEAD) gave its report in January 2004.[76]

The PIHEAD committee emphasized that globalization was a dominant feature of the twenty-first century because of which integration of societies was taking place. This had given rise to major challenges in interaction between individuals, groups, and even with nature. The gap between the rich and poor continued to widen both within the national boundaries and between nations. It was imperative that higher education offer solutions to existing challenges and innovate to avoid problems in the future. Whether in the economic, political, or social realms, higher education was expected to contribute to raising the overall quality of life, worldwide. It was felt that if higher education had to fulfil its role effectively and maintain excellence, it needed to become far more internationalized and integrate international and intercultural dimensions into teaching, research, and service functions. Preparing future leaders and citizens for a highly interdependent world required a higher education system that accepted cultural diversity and fostered intercultural understanding, respect, and tolerance. Thus it would contribute to building more than economically competitive and politically powerful regional blocks. Rather, it would help in creating a commitment to international solidarity, human security, to building a climate of global peace. The committee went on to enumerate advantages of the internalization of higher education in various areas like academic, social, cultural, political, and economic.

Among the academic advantages it was suggested that internationalization of higher education provided students access to learning materials, methodologies and teachers of the highest quality irrespective of national origin. It gave them an exposure to international curricula, and to practices in other systems of education. Further, it prepared students for an international employment market by familiarizing them with the dynamics of international sub-systems. Raising the quality of education by competition and through efforts to achieve international benchmarks, making research facilities of high order available to faculty and scholars through collaborative arrangements with other universities in particular and promoting both capacity-building and institution-building in general were some other advantages.[77]

Among the social-cultural advantages, the committee highlighted the benefits of a cosmopolitan environment that promoted understanding of different cultures and languages. In addition, it helped to develop a holistic approach that brought about the acceptance of the viewpoint of other societies, and thereby broadend the perception of individuals. The committee thought that it could also provide an opportunity to universities to add additional meaning to their social mission.[78]

Among the political benefits were the influences on the thought processes of future foreign leaders and decision-makers, which could not be ignored. Also, internalization of higher education enabled citizens of other countries to understand and appreciate the nation's priorities, needs and actions thereby enabling gains in international goodwill and raising the country's profile abroad. Economically, it helped in securing revenue for institutions from tuition fees, and for the larger society by providing services and in obtaining funds from international agencies. It could also help to develop expertise related to international relations, trade and management and promoting economic competitiveness.[79]

However, the committee realized that the Indian education system had not yet acquired the capacity to cope as it catered largely to domestic needs. Although India had certain advantages because of its low-cost delivery system, English as the medium of instruction, and its huge technological and management resources, it had not yet harnessed its immense potential of reaching out to foreign students. The inflow of foreign students in India was in a sorry state of affairs and unlike in the developed countries, the number of international students in India was going down. At the same time, the committee recognized that internationalization would necessarily be a relatively slow process as both institutions and individuals have to be made aware that cooperation with universities in different countries was beneficial to both. Above all, the stakeholders needed to understand that internationalization did not imply a dilution of the national culture and ethos, but actually resulted in the strengthening of these by learning from others. The committee then went on to detail the steps that had to be taken to make Indian higher education attractive abroad while at the same time strengthen it from within to build capacity to internationalize. It was realized that unlike some of the advanced English-speaking countries, particularly the USA, the UK, Canada and Australia that had made concerted efforts to attract international students, India had done little in this direction. Hence it was necessary to formulate a national policy and adopt consistent strategies that would encourage Indian institutions to admit international students. Currently, there were several constraints in the way of international students becoming a part of Indian university campuses. Under the present governmental policy, dictated in part by the apex court, educational institutions were permitted to admit a limited percentage of students to educational programmes in technical and professional fields. There was a need to seriously re-think this matter.[80]

Further, it was felt that a nodal agency would have to be created to coordinate the efforts and activities of Indian universities as they attempted to internationalize their education. This would mean establishing a Consortium for international education. The Consortium would identify select universities and institutions of higher learning, keeping in view standards, infrastructure and performance, so that a directory of centres of excellence could be prepared and updated where international students could be admitted. It could also help in projecting Indian universities/institutions in other countries and function on their behalf. Further, it could act as a clearing house for information on courses offered, availability of seats, the fee charged, the financial-assistance available, and possibility of on-campus housing accommodation for individuals and families. Publication and distribution of guides and handbooks for the promotion of international education programmes in the country was also a necessary function which could be performed by it. Coordinating education and training of international students of the universities/institutions of higher learning in the country and building a network, to liaise, collaborate and interact with relevant institutions, individuals and other agencies within and outside the country, to facilitate the promotion of international education cooperation programmes was another envisaged function.

The Consortium could also help Indian universities/ institutions of higher learning in obtaining approvals of the various ministries of the Government of India for different international education cooperation programmes by promoting, coordinating, and monitoring jointly the affairs of international students with the Indian universities/ institutions. It could also represent Indian universities/ institutions at International Fairs on Higher Education and organize similar fairs in India. It could further undertake, with the help of individuals and universities, ethnographic studies on international students to understand more about their experiences and also to make informed generalizations about specific nationality groups.

In addition to all these, the Consortium could also develop norms and guidelines for ensuring quality in international education and do all the other things which were incidental or conducive to the attainment of the main objects of any of them. The UGC was to oversee the credit system, semester system and teaching methods and for that, if required, the UGC Act could be amended to enable it to regulate foreign educational institutions in India. Similar exercises could be undertaken by the All India Council of Technical Education (AICTE) in respect of technical education. There was also focus on removing the procedural impediments in the way of opening Indian educational institutions abroad. But this was to be done carefully as substandard institutions could not be allowed to internationalize. This was important as there was an inherent danger that the reputation of the entire education system of the country could be spoilt.

To further the recommendation of the PIHEAD committee, the Committee for the Promotion of Indian Education Abroad (COPIE) was set up to suggest ways to promote Indian education abroad.[81] The committee decided to form two sub-committees. One was to be headed by the UGC Chairman, Chairman, AICTE, Director, National Assessment and Accreditation Council (NAAC); Secretary-General AIU, Chairman, CBSE and representatives of Confederation of Indian Industry (CII); Ministry of External Affairs(MEA); Indian Council of Agricultural Research (ICAR); and Ministry of Health, with the mandate to identify universities/courses with potential to attract foreign students; to improve their standards; and to promote Indian institutions in targeted countries through Indian Missions, Educational Consultant India Limited (ED.CIL). The second sub-committee was to be a standing committee of COPIE and to act as a clearing house for all proposals of Indian institutions either for setting up their campuses abroad or for entering into twinning arrangements with foreign educational institutions. The sub-committee was to receive all proposals from the Ministry of Human Resource Development (MHRD) and place them, along with their recommendations, before the COPIE for a final decision.

The deliberations of the committee give an impression that as far as the question of attracting foreign students to undertake degree and study programmes in Indian universities was concerned, there was a complete consensus on it. The committee, in addition, suggested that focused "Study India Programme" (SIP) in Indian universities for students from developed countries should be initiated. It also endorsed proposals such as (a) Initiation of "twinning" academic arrangements with foreign universities, (b) Setting up of foreign campuses of Indian universities, (c) Creation of special education zones for running of teaching and learning programmes exclusively for foreign students through Consortia of Indian Universities.[82]

The second sub-committee met on February 13, 2003 and gave comprehensive recommendations. It was of the view that the promotion of Indian education abroad should also include school education. The committee emphasized the need to accredit Indian educational institutions not only by NAAC but also by international accreditation agencies.[83] A natural precondition for internationalization was a uniform system of equivalence on the patterns of the universities of the West. This was also endorsed by the second subcommittee. The committee was of the opinion that since most Indian universities did not enjoy a good reputation internationally, they had to project themselves to attract foreign students. One way was to organize educational fairs in foreign countries. Universities/ courses could be identified and given wide publicity abroad through Indian embassies. Also, short-term courses specifically designed for foreign students could be introduced in select Indian universities. In addition to the Study India Programme, other important courses could also be identified which would attract foreign students to their campuses. But universities would have to make systemic changes as a first step. For example, the credit system together with the facility of credit transfer between institutions would have to be put into place. Further methods of evaluation within the various institutions had to be standardized to make them globally competitive. Other necessary changes were improved text material and teaching methods to get international recognition and accreditation.

The Committee felt that Indian education should initially target the African and South East Asian countries as they represented a client group distinct from Europe and the USA. Also, special efforts should be made to export education to the countries of the Middle East. However, an area that seems to have been overlooked by the committee was of Central Asia, particularly the former Soviet Republics which had the advantage of proximity and with whom India had historical, cultural, and civilization links. In all cases, apart from the other factors, the committee emphasized one great advantage that India had was that education was affordable.

The committee also touched on a very significant issue related to the supernumerary seats for the NRIs/PIOs, that the colleges/universities had been permitted to create. However, even these seats remained vacant in many institutions and this was of serious concern. Perhaps the rigidity in the admission system was a reason and to that extent it needed to be removed. The reputed institutions, the Committee suggested, should organize entrance tests in foreign countries also. At the same time bodies like the United States Education Foundation of India (USEFI), British Council and French, German and Australian Missions should be asked to give presentations on their educational programmes to understand and be familiar with their systems. It was recommended that the UGC should prepare a home page (a portal) on Indian education for foreign students and also brochures for distribution amongst them. Programmes such as SIP should be given priority over others. It was also decided that not only accredited institutions in the public sector but also reputed institutions of the private sector should be associated in this endeavour.

Following the recommendations of the PIHEAD committee, together with those of other committees, UGC together with some universities has been participating in the NAFSA conferences since 2004. The next NAFSA conference was held in May 2007 in Minneapolis, Minnesota, USA, its theme being "Preparing Global Citizens". Tied to the conference theme its Annual Conference Committee (ACC) has adopted five thematic threads to guide the creation of content for the conference. These are: (i) How does international education change our lives ? (ii) How does international education affect global development ? (iii) How are national, bi-national and regional policies affecting international education ? (iv) How can international educators work more effectively and creatively ? (v) What role do international educators play in global leadership ? However, while the Indian participation in the NAFSA conferences is an important step in the direction of internationalization of higher education, the question is whether the structure of higher education in India is ready for it. Unless the ground is prepared and systemic changes are made raising expectations at such a conference without the ability to deliver can be counter-productive and detrimental.

4

The Ground Realities

International Student Mobility

In spite of so many positive policy decisions and recommendations in the last few years from the Association of Indian Universities, the National University of Educational Planning and Development, and the University Grants Commission, the ground realities are that the population of foreign students is very small in India. This is when India has the third largest system of higher education in terms of enrolment after China and the USA.

One of the most important features of the second half of the twentieth century has been the gradual internationalization of higher education of which the most visible and important feature is trans-border student mobility. Building on the work of K.B. Powar, Sudhakar Pandey, Santosh Panda, Panda and Veena Bhalla, Pawan Agarwal maps the global trends of student mobility from 1990 to 2004. He finds that cross-border student mobility is in keeping with the growth of student enrolment. The enrolment of students in higher education increased globally by 40 per cent between 1999 and 2004 from

92 million to 132 million. During the same period the student mobility also increased by 41 per cent from 1.75 million to 2.5 million.[84]

The USA was the most popular destination with 23 per cent globally mobile students followed by UK, Germany, France and Australia with 12.2 per cent, 10.6 per cent, 9.7 per cent and 6.8 per cent respectively. The other major host countries were Japan (4.8%), China (4.8%), Russia (3.1%) and Canada (2.08%). Only a few developing countries like South Africa (2.5%) and Malaysia (1.1%) hosted a substantial number of international students. India has a mere half per cent of globally mobile students.[85]

As Powar points out and Agarwal substantiates, there are two dominant patterns of student mobility. The first is from developing countries to developed ones. The second is a more recent development of intra-regional movement. A large number of students move from one European country to another. Intra-Asian mobility too is increasing. This is also true of South America where 17 per cent of South American students sought international education experience in another South American University. Therefore, there has been an overall increase in student mobility and it has become more complex as a worldwide movement of students is taking place north-south, north-north, and south-south.[86]

Since English is now generally accepted as the international language of communication, the main English-speaking countries—USA, UK, Australia, Canada, and New Zealand—are the most favoured destinations and together host 50 per cent of all globally mobile students. This demand is expected to increase from 1 million places in 2003 to about 2.6 million places in 2020 with Asia contributing 76 per cent of this demand. Sensing an opportunity many non-English speaking countries like France, Sweden and Germany have also started programmes in English for globally mobile students. Traditional host countries now face competition from countries such as Singapore, Malaysia and UAE, especially since the setting up of the Knowledge City in Dubai.[87] Singapore increased its intake of international students from less then 50,000 in 2002 to 72,000 in 2005. Its target is to attract 150,000 international students by 2015. In addition, it is offering a number of concessions to prestigious foreign institutions to establish operations there. These include INSEAD from France, Cornell University, Duke University and the University of Chicago School of Business. It has been estimated by Bohm that as developing countries become wealthier and their population increases, the global demand for places in higher education would be 3.3 million in 2010 and 5.8 million in 2020.[88] Asia will continue to be the leading source again, accounting for 40 per cent of the total global demand in 2010.

The Indian Situation

As far as India is concerned, it gets international students from about 125 countries. As both Powar and Agarwal observe there are two categories of foreign students who come to India. The first belong to developed countries like the US, UK, Canada, Australia, countries of the European Union, and Japan that have very good facilities for higher education and training of their own. Students from these places come to India primarily for the cultural experiences. The second are those from less developed countries that have limited facilities for higher education and hence need to enrol in regular degree programmes.[89]

It is difficult to find the exact number of foreign students in India as the record-keeping in most universities is quite inadequate. Agarwal estimated 12,263 international students in higher education institutions in India in 2003-2004.[90] However, he felt that a better figure would be about 15,000 students given the lacunae in maintenance of records. And with an annual estimated growth of 8 per cent the number would be about 17,500 in 2005-2006. More than 90 per cent of the students came from the developing countries of Asia and Africa, with two-thirds coming from Asia and one-fourth from the African countries. Only 8 per cent came from other countries. Thirty per cent of students were from South and Central Asia and 20 per cent from North Africa and the Middle East. There were some students from the Caribbean and Latin America. Nepal sent the highest number of students to India followed by Bangladesh, Malaysia, Kenya, Sri Lanka, Iran, Mauritius, Ethiopia, the USA, and Oman. These were the top ten student-sending countries to India. This shows that the percentage of students from high income countries was extremely low in India.[91]

Doing a faculty-wise analysis of international students for the year 2003-2004, Agarwal's findings were that three-fourths of all international students were enrolled in Arts (28%), Sciences (26%) and Commerce (22%) There were about 72.53 per cent of students in undergraduate programmes and 17.8 per cent were doing postgraduation. Twenty-eight per cent of all students were girls. The number of students from developed countries was very small and they largely came for "short-term study abroad programmes" in order to get a cross-cultural experience.[92] Many advanced countries have instituted policies to encourage students to study abroad for a short time. This is especially true of the USA where Study Abroad is very popular. According to Open Doors 2006, the number of American students studying abroad reached 205,983, an increase of 8 per cent over the previous year.[93] It was also noted that the Study Abroad experience had moved ell beyond the typical "junior year abroad" as students increasingly sought educational experiences of various durations at different points in their academic career. They were also going increasingly to non-traditional destinations and to non-English speaking countries. There was a growing demand for China and India.

Open Doors lists the 20 most popular destinations for Study Abroad as: the United Kingdom, Italy, Spain, France, Australia, Mexico, Germany, China, Ireland, Costa Rica, Japan, Austria, New Zealand, Czech Republic, Greece, Chile, South Africa, Argentina, Brazil and India. Of these, only five are primarily English-speaking and most are located outside Western Europe. While 45 per cent of the US students were in the perennially popular destinations in Western Europe, such as the UK, Italy, Spain and France, there were major increases in the number of students going to other host countries. China, the only Asian country in the top ten preferred destinations, showed a 35 per cent increase, from 4,737 in 2005 to 6,389 in 2006. Although the growth in China's popularity was the most remarkable, several South American countries increasingly found favour. There were three new countries in the top twenty destinations for American students: Argentina, Brazil, and India. Study in Argentina increased 53 per cent to 2013 international students annually thus becoming the 18th most popular destination. Brazil at number 19 increased 20 per cent to 1994 students annually and India arrived at the 20th position with a 53 per cent to increase to 1767 annually.[94]

Analysis of data available at AIU for the last fifteen years done by both Veena Bhalla and Powar finds corroboration in Agarwal's study. It shows that from 1988-89, the number of international students coming to India increased steadily during the first half of the 1990s, reaching a peak of 13,000 students in 1993-94. After this, the numbers steadily declined in contravention to global trends, and a marked fall occurred in 1996-97. By the end of the millennium, the number had halved. It, however, revived again from 2001-2002.

Over 60 per cent of all international students in India are enrolled in just 10 out of the 274 universities that reported having international students. These are a mixture of both public and private institutions. The largest members attended the Manipal Academy of Higher Education, Bangalore University, University of Pune, and the University of Delhi. The other popular destinations, according to Agarwal, are Bharati Vidyapeeth and Symbiosis in Pune.[95] A random survey was done by the author as a part of the study.[96] While the above findings were largely substantiated, there were also other destinations that were found to be popular like the University of Mysore and the CMR Institutions in Bangalore. Largely, as Pawan Agarwal points out, students prefer metropolitan towns and the western and southern part of India. While the Manipal Academy of Higher Education (MAHE), Bharati Vidyapeeth and Symbiosis, all private deemed universities were actively recruiting foreign students, public-funded universities and colleges were generally more conservative. Perhaps the three exceptions were Universities of Pune, Bangalore, and Delhi together with their affiliated colleges. It was found during the survey done that most educational institutions did not have either the mind set or the organizational infrastructure to cope with foreign students in terms of physical space and human resource. The best equipped seemed the Manipal Academy of Higher Education (MAHE), CMR, and Osmania University.[3] Some more universities were making an effort to internationalize their campuses like the Sardar Patel University at Vallabh Vidyanagar but in others the number of foreign students had declined.

The Road Blocks

The question arises, what are the impediments in the way of international students coming to India? Some are obvious such as the paucity of institutions of higher education, lack of resources leading to inadequate physical and academic infrastructure and there being little or no consciousness in the majority of the institutions that diversity of student population is a desired goal to be actively pursued. When only about 7 to 11 per cent of India's eligible population has access to any kind of higher education, it implies that at least 90 per cent do not. As the Indian economy is strengthening, the domestic demand for higher education is increasing in India leading to higher enrolment numbers. This has been corroborated by the Knowledge Commission which has said that as compared to the 300 that exist today there should be 1500 universities by 2015 to achieve 15 per cent gross enrolment of the eligible population.[97] In the face of the dearth of institutes of higher education for the country's own requirements it seems a far cry to talk of accommodating and welcoming foreign students. The UGC prescribes 15 per cent seats in an academic institution for foreign students as supernumerary seats. This goal is nowhere near being achieved and understandably so given the all-round paucity of institutions in higher education.

There is not only a lack of institutions but also inadequate funding. According to Pawan Agarwal, developed countries like the UK, the USA, Australia, Germany, France, Canada, and most Scandinavian countries spend over 1 per cent of their GDP on higher education. Amongst the developed countries, Japan and Korea are the exceptions, spending only 0.54 and 0.34 per cent respectively of their GDP on higher education but in these countries, over 80 per cent of the enrolled students are in unsubsidized private higher education institutions. In the USA, while 66 per cent of expenditure on higher education comes from private sources, public expenditure, too, is very high, being 1.41 per cent of its GDP. The developing countries usually spend less than 0.5 per cent of their GDP on higher education. India, too spends less than half per cent on higher education, while the recommendation is that it should spend 1.5 per cent of GDP out of a total of at least 6 per cent of GDP for education overall. It was felt that even this may not suffice for the massive expansion of higher education that is required, in which case, other possibilities can be explored to complement the increase in public expenditure. Further, even the small amount that is spent on higher education is very unevenly distributed. Nearly one-third of the institutions do not get any government funds. Of the remaining, only about half get Central funding. The small number of institutions that cater to less than 2 per cent of the students get 85 per cent of the Central funds. The rest receive pitifully small amounts of Central funds and have to depend on the state governments for funding. Many of them are in perpetual financial problems. This is not healthy for higher education itself and also makes it much less feasible to attract foreign students.

Perhaps it is some of these factors that have led to the lack of student mobility in India so that there is little diversity on university campuses, especially of state universities. This is evident from a survey done by Pawan Agarwal on the geographical diversity of students in India on university campuses.[98] Four factors were looked at: the percentage of students from within the state where the institution is located; from the neighbouring states, from other states; and the percentage of foreign students. One hundred and sixteen institutions, both professional and non-professional, responded. The average worked out to about 69.1 per cent students being from within the state; about 12.8 per cent being from neighbouring states; about 17 per cent being from other states and about 1.3 per cent being foreign students. A closer analysis reveals little or no student diversity in non-professional institutions. The regional professional institutions also had little student diversity but national professional institutions that conducted a national level entrance exam showed a fair degree of student diversity. The number of foreign students in all institutions was negligible.

However, university campuses must have student diversity as a desired goal, especially in a country like India with its variety of languages, customs, traditions, religions, music, dance, and other ways of life. Multicultural and diverse campuses are more dynamic and vibrant than the more homogeneous ones. Diversity, of student population in Indian universities reflecting the different regions of India would be an effective way of developing inter-regional understanding among young people. Their interpersonal skills would improve and horizons widened, making them more cosmopolitan rather than parochial and rigid. This is the first step that needs to be taken before internationalization can become effective. It is not strange, then, for foreign students to prefer institutions in metropolitan towns where there is a greater acceptance of student diversity, more amenities and where they can integrate more easily on the university campuses.

In this context, it might be useful to remember that one fact of today's globalized world is not just student mobility. There is also global trade in higher education that is constantly growing. The Organization for Economic Cooperation and Development (OECD) estimated this to be more than $30 billion per annum in 2000. According to Merrill Lynch, the size of the international education market was estimated at 2 trillion dollars in 1999.[99] The 2005 US Open Doors Report estimated that international students contributed over 13 billion dollars to the US economy in 2005. It rose further in 2006 and the contribution was $13,499,404,249.[100] The USA is in fact the biggest exporter of educational services followed by the UK, Australia, Italy, and Canada, as many students see these countries as their educational destinations and the countries earn revenue because of it. It was the largest importer of educational services followed by Italy, Canada, Australia, and the UK as many of their students spend some time during their degree programmes in other countries at a lower cost. All the major exporters of education were developed countries, while developing countries like China, India, the Philippines and Indonesia were major importers of the service. India, it may be noted, sent the highest number of students to the USA. Currently, over 80,000 Indian students were studying in America. Besides the USA, Indian students were going to the UK, Australia, Canada and now even to Singapore and the Knowledge City of Dubai. The total number could be an estimated 150,000 students. The outflow of foreign exchange from India is estimated to be 4 billion dollars annually on higher education. [101] Thus obviously countries encouraged cross-border higher education not for altruistic reasons alone but to also earn valuable revenue for their institutions. The inflow of foreign students also benefited the economy as they lived and travelled in that country and often returned to it. In their wake came their families and friends and often more students if the experience was an enriching one. Such an inflow of students not only establishes the reputation of the educational institutions but also makes them more vibrant and dynamic as they internationalize syllabi and curricula, and increase and upgrade infrastructure, both physical and academic, for which resources become more readily available.

The Field Study

As a part of this study the author administered a questionnaire to both current students and alumni to find out about their educational experience in India.[4] To begin with, it was rather difficult to reach the foreign students as most institutions did not have enough organizational infrastructure to keep records and to track them. In some places, like Gujarat, there were security apprehensions about responding to the questionnaire. Finally, 429 responses were received from current international students studying mainly in the western and southern parts of India. One hundred and eleven alumni responses were also received. The bulk of these were from developing countries such as Afghanistan, Thailand, Bangladesh, Sri Lanka, Bhutan, Fiji, Ethiopia, Malaysia, Tanzania, Kenya, Mauritius, Sudan, Maldives, Nepal, Sri Lanka, Oman, Kenya, Korea, Tajikistan, Uzbekistan, Yemen, Vietnam, Iran, Indonesia, Mongolia, Syria, Turkmenistan, and

Yemen. A few came from developed countries such as the USA, Australia, Canada, France, and Germany. Most of the latter were obviously of Indian origin studying mainly in professional courses of MBBS and BDS. There was a very large proportion of Malaysian students in medical courses because of the twinning arrangement between the medical school of Manipal Academy of Higher Education and its medical school in Malacca. However, these can only be taken as indicators as the survey is by no means exhaustive.

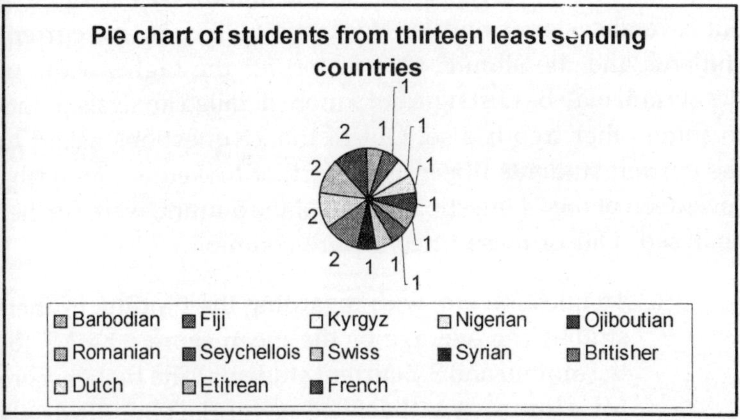

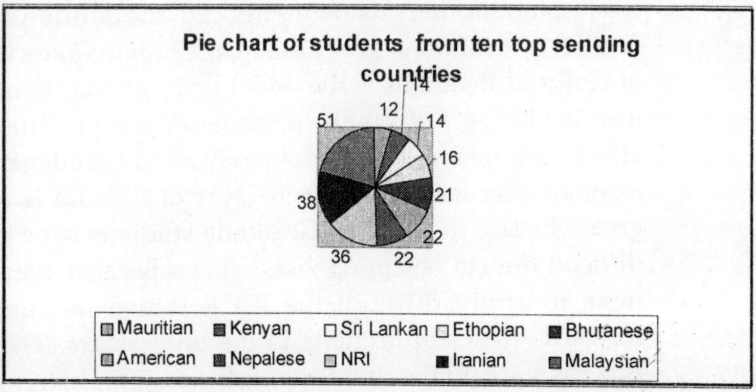

Both the current students and the alumni had the option of not answering any or some of the questions, if they so wished. The questions were then graded on a scale of five. The most satisfactory answers were given five points. The satisfactory ones were given four points, the dissatisfied ones were given three, and the very dissatisfied ones, two. The blank answers were given one. There were 21 questions for the current students and 24 for the alumni, the three extra being concerned with the experiences of the alumni as they looked back upon them. The overall response to Indian education both of current students and alumni was favourable but several systemic hurdles also came to light by the current students and the alumni. One factor, for the higher score of the alumni may be nostalgia but a more detailed analysis points to some other trends also. Out of the 21 questions asked to the current students fifteen were further looked at. Similarly, seventeen of the 24 questions asked of the alumni, were further analysed. Out of these fifteen, were common.

1. To question one with regarding the funding of their studies the average or the mean score was 3.7 for the alumni and 3.1 current students. The higher score for alumni was because several ITEC students responded who are fully funded by the government of India. That means that the bulk of the students were either self-financed or received some funding from their home governments. Of the students funded by the Indian government, the Indian Council of Cultural Relations is the nodal body giving them grants. These are given in terms of quota. This effectively means that it does not attract students from all over the world. Then, issue of the visa is a great obstacle in the way. Generally students have a difficult time in obtaining visas. This is because they have to apply through the ICCR which in turn forwards their applications to the universities. The process starts in the months of February and March.

By the time the universities respond it is already time to begin the course and in many cases the students are left with little or no time to plan their trip. The case gets further complicated in case of PhD students where the approval of the MHRD is additionally required.

2. The next question, number two was concerning how the foreign students had found out about Indian institutions. The highest mark was given if both the Indian missions abroad and the student's home government had information about the institutions and courses available in India. Then, the responses were graded according to whether only the Indian missions provided the information or if it was available only with the students' own government. The two lowest scores were if the information was obtained only through some other sources like acquaintances or relatives and which could or could not be corroborated by the home government or the Indian mission with ease. The mean score was 4.02 for the alumni and 3.65 for the current students. This indicates that most Indian missions disseminated the information. In addition, students got information through their own sources like friends and relatives who had studied in India or from their own government. The Indian embassies abroad do have handbooks that contain information about courses and universities but the fact remains that these embassies are not situated in all the major areas. This effectively means that Indian universities remain largely inaccessible to the foreign students. Further the lack of integrated sites on the internet providing comprehensible information to the students is a major obstacle in the way. The ICCR gets the application forms and sends it to some

universities but inadequate coordinating mechanisms severely limit the chances.

3. In respect to question three as to how they decided on their present educational institution the mean score was 3.74 and 4.08 respectively for the current students and the alumni respectively indicating that most of them were allotted a course and an institution according to their availability. The mean score for current students is lower than that for the alumni. This might indicate that there was greater availability of courses and institutions earlier than at present. This could be because of inertia both at the university and the bureaucratic level and also because of higher domestic demand with which the higher education infrastructure has not managed to keep pace.

4. Regarding their course of study, in question four the mean for both the alumni and current students was 4.25. This means that they were on the whole satisfied with the contents of the course. However, to be really at the top, the universities have not only to fine tune the content of the courses available but also to make the grading and the examination system attuned to the internationally prevailing norms. Further, the courses need to be restructured giving enough flexibility to the students. It cannot be forgotten that the bulk of the students are from developing countries where facilities for higher education are inadequate. But these countries are also catching up and unless Indian universities keep up with the best in content and pedagogy, they are gradually likely to become less attractive. A good example is that of Singapore, Malaysia and the UAE. These countries are making organized efforts to attract reputed foreign universities to their countries.

UAE has established a knowledge city that has the presence of good foreign universities including institutions like BITS Pilani. It can lead to a piquant situation of an Indian educational institution set up abroad attracting Indian students from India who pay a much higher fee leading to both flight of talent and outflow of foreign exchange. Singapore is on its way to becoming a trusted education hub and in the process is attracting a large number of foreign students. Its intake of foreign students has increased from 50,000 in 2002 to 70,000 in 2005. The target is 1,50,000 by 2015 which would create 22,000 jobs in Singapore's economy and increase the education sector's GDP contribution from 1.9 per cent or 1.8 billion dollars to 5 per cent. It is offering concessions to reputed foreign universities and has set up an Education Excellence Framework (EEF) that focuses on education and organizational excellence, and good student protection and welfare practices.

5. The students interviewed were also asked about their preference for a particular city/town in India and the reasons for it in question five. The mean score of 4.25 for the current and 3.94 for the alumni suggests that they were satisfied with what they got. However, the bulk of students were assigned the institutions and they really had no preference of their own. Greater information to a potential candidate would lead to choices rather than just accepting what is being offered.

6. Regarding their place of stay in question six, the mean was 4.27 and 4.33 for the current students and the alumni respectively indicating that by and large, they did manage to get hostel accommodation. The highest marks were given for stay in a hostel. The

slightly lower mean for current students might indicate that hostel accommodation was shrinking. It has to be remembered that the number of foreign students is currently very small. If the numbers increase, more hostel accommodation would have to be made available. Also, Indian universities suffer from lack of resources. This has meant that the existing hostel facilities have not been continuously upgraded.

7. When asked about experiences in the first week of their arrival the mean score of 3.05 for the current students and 3.27 for the alumni does not present a happy picture. It indicates their dissatisfaction, that is, they had a tough time on their arrival. This is obvious because most educational institutions are not organized enough to help international students. Usually these students (with some exceptions) had to fend for themselves even for their small day-to-day needs in the initial settling down period. There were also problems like difficulties in opening bank accounts, inadequate information about transportation, no ready availability of things like the roadmap of the town and others that made settling down in the first few days difficult. Creating a student-friendly atmosphere is essential and does not require a great amount of resources. It is more a mind set. A little bit of thought can go a long way into making the initial period easier. It was also seen that many international students came from countries where English was not the medium of instruction. Thus communication became a problem not only with fellow students but also in following the courses being taught. Introducing intensive short duration English language teaching programmes could ease both peer group interaction and academic difficulties because of language.

8. When asked about the time they took to settle down physically in India the mean score of 3.34 for the current students and 3.30 for the alumni suggests that they took a fairly long time. The reasons could be similar to those given in the context of the previous question.

9. Similarly, on the issue of feeling at home the average score of the alumni was 3.65 and 3.25 for current students. Again this conforms to the findings of the earlier questions and indicates their discomfort in India. The slightly higher score of alumni could be because of an element of nostalgia and also because they may have been better looked after. The pace of life has quickened and Indian students show a greater preoccupation with their own careers. This may leave them less time for befriending international students. This is borne out by the scores in the next question dealing with peer group interaction. The policy makers, too, paid more attention to them. For example, Jawaharlal Nehru used to meet them personally and many of them even stayed with Members of Parliament. Today, ministers whether in the Ministry of External Affairs or Human Resource Development have little time for them. However, this may not even be necessary if the university system had a structure in place that gave due importance to internationalization of education and recognized its relevance. It has to be remembered that foreign students can go back as friends or the experience can be a bad one. Both have an impact when these students get into decision-making positions.

10. The students were also asked about their peer group interactions. Interestingly, the mean score of 3.95 for the alumni and 3.28 for the current students

indicates that the alumni had better peer interaction than the current students who often appear to feel either alienated or lost.

11. An average score of 4.44 and 3.94 for the alumni and the current students respectively on the issue of satisfaction and usefulness of the course that they pursued suggests that the foreign students found these courses more useful earlier than now. The level of satisfaction was higher in professional courses than in the non-professional ones. It was particularly good in the case of ITEC students who were more mature and were here on short-term programmes particularly useful for their specific needs. Their responses showed much higher levels of appreciation than those of regular degree students.

12. In terms of comparing the courses that the foreign students were pursuing with similar courses in their own country, especially in terms of cost, curriculum structure and professional management, an average score of 3.51 and 3.87 for the current students and alumni respectively suggests that they feel that they are just or slightly better. The higher score of the alumni indicates that Indian courses compared more favourably than now. This is because education in the source countries is improving and Indians will have to keep pace to maintain their academic and pedagogic edge.

13. To gauge the satisfaction with the course that these students were pursuing they were asked whether they would have preferred pursuing some other course instead of the current one and the reason for that. The answer here threw an average of 3.66 for the current and 4.48 for the alumni. This suggests that they were fairly satisfied with the courses they

were pursuing. However, the level of satisfaction seems to have been much higher in the alumni. This is in keeping with the finding in the previous question in which too the alumni were more satisfied. Here, after the nostalgia is factored in, one reason could be that in contemporary situations, Indian institutions need to have more innovative courses. But here a distinction has to be made between professional courses for which students came under programmes like the ITEC and the undergraduate courses pursued in the various universities. The professional courses evinced greater satisfaction than others.

14. The average score of 3.96 for the current students and 4.44 for the alumni on the issue of whether they would recommend more students from their country suggests the continuing interests of foreign students studying in India. However, as in the previous two questions, the alumni seem happier to recommend to others to study in India than the current students. (Question 17 for current students and 18 for Alumni). Again, the variation needs to be factored in for the alumni for nostalgia, but the potential is there. India only needs to capitalize on it. Also, the higher score for alumni could be because they studied in days when the education environment in their own countries was different and the expectations from the education system were lower. As the Mauritian High Commissioner, Shri Mookhesswur Choonee, himself an alumnus of three universities in India, pointed out, educational opportunities in Mauritius had also increased and many of these institutions were also entering into collaborative arrangements with reputed Western universities. Also, he felt, that the affluence of the Mauritians had increased. Hence,

the more affluent preferred Western destinations where he educational standards were perceived to be higher and there were also no problems with the recognition of their degrees. The others were increasingly finding opportunities at home. This had led to a decline in the numbers of Mauritian students coming to India. While Indian universities provided good education at a much lower cost, they would have to reach international standards and solve the problem of recognition of degrees if they wanted to compete globally and attract foreign students. This view was in keeping with the findings about the situation in Singapore discussed earlier.

15. The alumni were asked in question sixteen about the impact on them of their stay in India. A score of 4.17 indicated that the experience was a fairly powerful one. During the interaction with them, most of them used the word 'transformational'. Many have written as much. They learnt to understand and enjoy a different culture, found the courses professionally useful and made lifelong friends in India with many of whom contact at both professional and family level has remained.

16. The response of 4.40 and 3.52 for the alumni and current students to the question whether education played a role in promoting relations between the countries is thought-provoking. (Question 23 for alumni and 20 for current students). A higher appreciation of the role of education in public diplomacy among alumni could be because of greater maturity levels. However, the variation can also alert us to the fact that foreign students can return as goodwill ambassadors or become indifferent or even negative if the experience is not a rewarding one. Hence, it is essential to make the education system

more responsive to dealing with foreign students if it has to produce the desired outcomes.

India's External Relations and the Education Sector

It would be useful to examine how education cooperation can help India's foreign policy objectives. High priority has always been accorded to relations with neighbours. There is already a fair amount of cooperation with most of the SAARC countries except Pakistan. Recognizing the importance of education in promoting regional cooperation, India had proposed the establishment of SAARC University during the last summit at Dhaka. It would be useful to accelerate the decision-making process for early fruition of the idea. Apart from this, India must take the lead in promoting student and faculty exchange programmes with universities in SAARC countries.

Nepal and Bhutan already enjoy a special status in Indian universities. Students from these countries, for example, are eligible to get admission in Delhi University even on scoring 5 per cent less than the basic eligibility for Indian students. India being the education destination for the people of Nepal has played a positive role in their bilateral relations. But it has not been possible to accommodate the demand of a large number of Nepalese students particularly for professional courses. Seeing this need the Manipal Academy of Higher Education (MAHE) has opened a Medical College in Nepal. Unfortunately its full potential has not been realized because of political turbulence there. In a deemed university like MAHE, the Nepalese students could have been accommodated in India itself but excessive regulatory framework in India made Nepal a more attractive destination. The institution in Nepal also attracts students from India and some other foreign countries.

India is the first choice destination for higher education for the Bhutanese who look to it to play a significant role in the development of human resources in their own country. Bhutanese society is gradually opening up and education there is bound to grow. It is essential that India play a key role in helping educationally in Human Resource Development and thus shaping attitudes towards India in a newly democratic Bhutan.

With regard to Sri Lanka, while education is playing a positive role in the development of bilateral relations between the two countries, its full potential has not been realized because of paucity of seats and institutions in India. Apart from general education, Buddhist studies need to be paid greater attention. A number of Sri Lankans come to study Buddhism in India. It is necessary to remember that the Buddhist clergy plays an important role in Sri Lanka's national affairs. Special attention should be paid to Buddhist studies also because of the large number of Buddhist countries in the world who expect India to provide the lead in areas of philosophy and comparative religion. There is only one centre of Buddhist studies in Varanasi but many more can be developed and departments of philosophy need to be strengthened.

With the neighbours on the east and west of its borders there are little or no educational linkages. There is some cooperation with Bangladesh in the field of Higher Education but could be improved and strengthened. Bangladesh sends a large number of students to India but India is unable to meet the huge demand for professional and vocational courses from Bangladesh students. There is hardly any faculty exchange among universities in Bangladesh and Indian Universities and few if any joint research projects. Such initiatives would not only enhance cooperation in the field of education but also help develop better understanding. Owing to linguistic commonality it should be possible to develop close linkages between academic institutions of the two countries.

especially with universities in West Bengal. With Pakistan this areas has been a closed one. As part of confidence-building measures, it would be worthwhile to begin with small steps like faculty exchange in this field.

The greatest expectation of Afghanistan from India is help in creating human resource for the reconstruction of its war-ravaged country including education facilities. The government has realized the importance of education in promoting Indo-Afghan relations and has started special schemes for the training of Afghan students in India. This is a challenge because war has interrupted the educational processes there and created imbalances in societal structures, but if India can meet it, it will be an important aspect of India's cultural diplomacy towards these strategically important neighbours. The Prime Minister of India has offered massive aid in human resource development to Afghanistan. Even earlier, a number of Afghans have studied in India including President Hamid Karzai. The impact of his educational experience in India was visible in the affection with which he remembered his teachers at the Himachal Pradesh University in Shimla from where he did his postgraduation in Political Science.[102]

India's cultural relations with Southeast Asia is one of the most fascinating fields of history This interaction goes back over two thousand years and has left a lasting impact on almost every aspect of life in a number of countries of the region. The most unique feature of this interaction is that it has been entirely peaceful. There is probably no other example in history of such cross-fertilization between different cultures and people for over two millennia without any involvement of military force. Former Prime Minister Narasimha Rao's "Look East" Policy was a major foreign policy initiative in the post Cold War era. Relations with ASEAN is the cornerstone of the "Look East" Policy. Recognizing the close cultural ties between the two regions, India had also taken the initiative of launching "Ganga-Mekong Partnership" with the ASEAN countries of the region.

Education too has played an important role in India's relationship with a number of Southeast Asian countries since India's independence particularly Malaysia, Thailand, and Singapore. With the other countries of the region, stronger educational links can be built. A large number of Indian teachers teach in Brunei but there is little or no educational contact with Philippines and Indonesia. A few Indonesian students have come to India on ITEC and ICCR scholarships but keeping in view the large population of the country and its growing needs for skilled human resource, this relationship can be developed.

A large number of Malaysian students came to study in India till the end of the 1980s. Many of them went on to occupy high positions in Malaysian society. These students played an important role in the all-round development of Indo-Malaysian relations. Malaysian University Graduate Association (MAYUG), an association of university graduates from India, has been active in promoting Indo-Malaysian ties. They have made a mark in academics, law and engineering. A large majority of doctors in Malaysia have been trained in India. However the number of students has declined since the early 1990s. A meeting with some alumni indicated several reasons for this. One is that Malaysia has developed its own institutions. Alternate destinations such as Australia, New Zealand, and Singapore have also emerged. With growing affluence bright Malaysian students have started enrolling in larger numbers in universities in the USA and UK. Also, there have been problems of equivalence and recognition of Indian degrees which have not been addressed by India. On the contrary because of pressures on Indian institutions, these have become more inward-looking. The Indian regulatory framework has also contributed to these declines. The consequence has been that institutions like MAHE have opened a campus in Malacca to overcome the difficulties created by the rigid regulatory framework of higher education in India. However, discussions with a number of Malaysian academics and other members of the civil society make it evident that interest in Indian higher education remains. Only a more proactive policy in India is required.

There has been close cooperation between India and Thailand in higher education since Indian independence. The situation in recent years is somewhat similar to that of Malaysia. Discussions with Indian alumni as well as their academics show it is possible to revive the relationship provided India pursues it. People of Indian origin in Thailand have a particularly strong interest in quality education in India. It is interesting that Shivnath Rai Bajaj has given an endowment of 1 million baht to start an India Study Centre at the Thammasat University.

A number of students from Singapore came to study in India till they developed their own high quality educational infrastructure. Currently, the majority of Singapore students who go abroad now prefer universities in the developed world, particularly the USA. The Singapore government, too, is vigorously developing the country as a destination of higher education. However, they are still keen to collaborate with India as can be seen from the initiatives taken for a campus of IIM, Bangalore in Singapore. They are also keen to have linkages with the IITs. Singapore is keen on student exchange programmes and has been interacting with good Indian universities like Delhi University.[103]

Vietnam, Cambodia, and Laos form a group like the Southeast Asian countries that have had close cultural links with India. Vietnam is a strategic partner in the ASEAN. They look upon India to play a major role in the development of its human resource. It is amongst the highest recipients of ITEC fellowships and are particularly keen for cooperation in the field of IT Education. The National Institute of Information Technology (NIIT) has established its presence in Vietnam. Some self-financing Vietnamese students have also started coming to India for management and other professional education. Given the high growth rate of Vietnam's economy, the trend could grow further. That educational stay leaves a lasting impact is evident from the warm and emotional speech of the Foreign Minister of Vietnam, Nguyen Dy Nien on his being conferred a doctorate by his alma mater, the Banaras Hindu University:

> When I came here 40 years ago, this country was like an Egyptian Sphinx's puzzle to me. It was a fresh world that aroused my curiosity and passion. It was also a world filled with mysteries that were hard to fathom. I learnt Hindi. I bathed in the holy water of the Ganges. I chatted and became acquainted with Indian friends, and travelled to almost every state to discover India. I managed to get into the world of Premchand and Tagore's poetry and literature and traced back Indian history through Nehru's writings. I read Gandhi's writings to learn about Ahimsa, I studied Radhakrishnan's works to understand a little bit about Indian philosophy and found out the links between India and Vietnam. India's culture, history, religions, and philosophy were so appealing and interesting to me. I led a life as a real Indian in a diverse and distinctive culture, which is home to one of the brightest civilizations of mankind. Later on, wherever I am in Vietnam or elsewhere in the world, those days continue to serve as a link between India and myself.

The position of Laos and Cambodia is somewhat similar to that of Vietnam. Given the cultural affinity with these countries, there is room for strong linkages with them in the field of education.

Central Asia is another region with which India has had strong civilization and cultural links. India also enjoyed considerable goodwill with many countries that formed a part of the earlier Soviet Union. These countries are in a state of transition. Their most important requirement is the development of human resource. Because of traditional links and the respect that India enjoys as a knowledge economy, they are keen on India's assistance in the field of education. Geographic proximity and affordability are important factors in favour of India. Some students from the former Soviet Republics have started coming to India mostly on ICCR and ITEC fellowships. However, these countries would have a growing middle-class community in the coming years which would be keen on quality education. This would create further opportunities for collaboration in the education sector and could lead to the strengthening of ties. Even the former Soviet Union had used education as an important tool of diplomacy, particularly in its relations with developing India. Many Indian scientists and doctors were trained in the erstwhile Soviet Union.

Like South East Asia and Central Asia, India also has traditional ties with Western Asia. A number of students from Iran, and the Arab and Gulf countries have studied in India. Many Arab students would look towards India if quality education was available because culturally they feel more comfortable here than in the West, especially after the September 11 tragedy in the USA. They look at other options and India is necessarily one of them. Collaboration in education would ensure that the traditional people-to-people contacts between India and West Asia are not only continued but further strengthened. Though the rich students of course prefer to study in Europe and America, Dubai has realized the potential of providing quality higher education and so has taken the initiative to establish a Knowledge City to meet the educational needs of the region. There was a similar recommendation in the Report of the High Level Committee *to establish Special Education Zones in India but not much thought has been given to the idea. Ironically many Indian institutions have started setting up campuses in the Knowledge City. Some of the Indian institutions already there are BITS Pilani, Mahatma Gandhi Institute, and Manipal Academy of Higher Education. As a result, some students from India, too, have started enrolling in these campuses. India's loss of opportunity could be Dubai's gain. The trend is likely to grow in the coming years.

Africa has always been special to India because of their common struggle against colonialism. The architect of India's foreign policy, Jawaharlal Nehru, accorded a very high priority to relations with Africa. Under this policy, India extended scholarships to a large number of African students. Several of them went on to hold important positions in their own countries. For example, Salim Ahmad Salim who did his undergraduate studies from Delhi University was Foreign Minister of Tanzania and later Prime Minister and Secretary of the Organization of the African Union (OAU) for a very long time, from 1989-2001. The educational support given by India generated enormous goodwill for the country among African leaders. Unfortunately because of inadequate follow up and lack of a proper institutionalized mechanism, both India and Africa could not realize the full potential of this aspect of their relationship. Human resource remains a major constraint in African development efforts. Except in South Africa, the educational infrastructure of most countries of the continent remains most inadequate. The leaders realize the need for the development of education for quality human resource. India can help and this can be a major factor in Indo-African ties.

The Indian economy has gained strength and the country has made a mark in areas like Information Technology and Biotechnology. India is progressively being recognized as a knowledge society and a country that needs to be studied and understood. This has awakened the interest of developed countries. Of course, it has also to be acknowledged that the internet is not just an academic or a cultural one. A prosperous Indian middle class looking for opportunities and excellence in higher education together with global opportunities has also made at least the metropolitan cities a fair hunting ground for recruiting full-fee paying students for many universities from developed countries. As has been seen, education has also become a trade with vast economic benefits both to education institutions and to the country's economy as a whole. The situation has been aggravated by the paucity of seats in good educational institutions in India. But that apart, students from developed countries want to come on short-term programmes for gaining some understanding of the country and a first hand cultural experience as it is useful for developing economic and political linkages. Relations with the European Union are high on India's foreign policy agenda. Both India and Europe recognize the potential role of education in the development of both bilateral and Indo-EU relations; India and the UK have historical ties and at one time the UK used to be the education destination for elite Indians. That has been replaced by the USA but during his visit to India, Gordon Brown, the then Chancellor of the Exchequer and now Prime Minister announced the setting up of an educational fund to ensure cooperation in this field. France and Germany too are beginning to look into student exchange programmes with India.

Similarly with the USA, as has already been discussed, India has had long-standing ties that kept a dialogue of academics and thinkers in place even during the height of the Cold War. Cultural and educational diplomacy as an exercise of soft power declined in the US after the disintegration of the Soviet Union but events of September 11 and the Iraq War have once again brought it to the fore. Besides, the growing Indian economy and closer political Indo-American ties have created an interest in India among American universities. The most effective and popular mode of academic collaboration is that of exchange programmes at various levels.

To meet this growing need, UGC had initiated the Study Abroad Programme.[104] However, its implementation has not taken off to any large extent because of the bottlenecks discussed earlier. There are academic constraints. The student exchange programmes have had an uneven implementation and in very few universities. Unless Indian universities move to the semester system and credit-based programmes, they will not have the required flexibility to participate in short-term student exchange programmes. The first step is to put these into place. The student exchange programme have had an uneven implementation and in very few universities. Apart from systemic academic impediments, universities lack awareness of academic, societal and economic benefits. Hence a consequence of all these factors is resistance in the university system. This has to be overcome.

The Way Forward

Therefore the education sector is an effective and unobtrusive mode of creating a proper understanding of India among young people. The developing world looks to India to take a lead in helping them to develop their own human resource. With the economic growth of India in a democratic framework, the developed world is interested in understanding the country through student exchange programmes and faculty and research linkages. The diaspora wants to understand and retain its cultural heritage. It looks to India to create opportunities for doing so in addition to normal academic exchange and linkages in which too it can help. Education should, then, be an integral part of economic assistance given by India to the developing countries. It has the expertise, the cultural understanding and environment, together with the educational infrastructure that has the potential to deliver. However, the university system does not have much sensitivity to this aspect so there is minimal motivation to act. Besides the system itself has problems of both numbers and resources creating its own challenges. Hence, when it is called upon to provide for one more sector, it responds with fatigue and inertia. So what can be done?

As has been pointed out, the bulk of students coming to India are from developing countries. While most of the higher education sector in India has still to reach international standards, at the same time India has also emerged as a country with a highly talented pool of educated people that have played a pivotal role in developing India's technology and economy. Professionals from India have made their mark all over the world competing with the best. Indian education is attractive to developing countries because it is affordable and the societal environment is more conducive for their students than that of the West. Besides, India's own policies have been to provide human resource development to developing countries that has given it leadership amongst them. However, most of the initiatives have come from the Ministry of External Affairs. The first step is for the MEA to take measures to sensitize institutions like the UGC, NUEPA and the AIU. Through them it must hold a series of events like workshops and seminars in universities and professional institutions to create awareness about this dimension of higher education as that alone will ensure effective and convincing implementation. Perhaps the Policy Planning division and the ICCR can develop linkages with these organizations.

In interactions during the field study, the response in several universities was that foreign students bring with them a host of problems and challenges and there was no reason why the institutions should first admit them and then deal with their problems. In any case there was such a huge domestic demand for higher education that could not be met was the argument, so why share the limited resources both physical and academic, with outsiders ? Even resource generation was not much of a motivation because government policies gave no incentive to do so. On the contrary, they were usually discouraging and there were disincentives. Even where research linkages were sought to be established, barring a few institutions, most of them were individual efforts and Memoranda of Understanding remained only on paper because of no clear policies and resources.

Therefore the Ministry of External Affairs needs to create a sensitivity and understanding of this dimension of education among other agencies like the Ministry of Human Resources Development, University Grants Commission and the Universities themselves. But it has to see it as a priority for itself before it can convince others. From the responses received from foreign students, the ITEC students appeared to be more satisfied than the others. Perhaps this is because they are more mature and are professionals. Also, they are better looked after, the nature of their programme being different from that of students who go to regular universities. They are also able to visit a few places in India as part of their programme which gives them a first hand experience of the cultural wealth of India. At least for the ICCR scholarship holders, a short trip to some places can be made an integral part of their programme. In addition just as the ITEC students have an ITEC day declared by the Ministry of External Affairs on which the embassies organize an event for ITEC students of their region to ensure continued association, the missions abroad must keep in touch with those who have studied in India and resources need to be made available for that. This would ensure better record keeping and lead to continual contact useful for both.

Once the Ministry of External Affairs begins to emphasize education and its consequent soft power benefits, it must draw up a calendar of events to sensitize others. It needs to collaboratively hold seminars and other academic events with institutions like NUEPA and the various departments in universities, both Central and State, especially where Foreign Students' advisors are already there. Unless there is sensitivity in education administration and faculty members the ground cannot be prepared for implementation.

The argument will be that most universities face a resource crunch both physical and academic because of which they are not able to cope with domestic demand. In such a situation, how can they be asked to accept foreign students ? This however, is not unique to the education sector. In spite of domestic requirements, India gives aid and assistance in different forms to various countries and institutions. It also makes investments that are not necessarily of import to immediate societal amelioration. If it is accepted as policy that the education sector is significant in contributing to India's external relations, adequate provision will have to be made for it. In any case, even for domestic requirements more resources have to be made available to the higher education sector. The Kothari Commission had recommended 6 per cent of GDP to be spent on education, which has not happened even sixty years after independence. Of this, at least 1 to 2 per cent must be spent on higher education as the developed nations do, whereas India spends only about 0.5 per cent. Apart from the much acclaimed IITs and IIMs, the Indian education system is complex and uneven in standards. However, over 88 per cent of education takes place in the 300 universities and over 18,000 colleges spread across the country.

It is imperative to improve standards and evolve a credible accreditation system. This is important for both domestic requirements and for internationalization of education.

The internationalization of education has already been accepted as a desired goal both by the Universities in the Mysore statement and the subsequent Guru Nanak University Conference. The UGC has recommended a 15 per cent intake of foreign students over and above the sanctioned seats in every educational institution. It was a thrust area for the UGC in the Tenth Plan and the several initiatives were taken. However, financial allocations have to be done to make this recommendation of the UGC a reality. It must also strive to improve standards of educational institutions and do all that is required to this end. In any case, all foreign students are not to be given scholarships or financed by India. Many of them are self-financing and actually contribute additional resources where they are enrolled. This is evident from the experience of universities like the University of Pune and from the deemed universities who are more proactive in this regard

Further, it is necessary to see diversity as a desired goal of universities. Except for professional institutions that hold national entrance examinations in most universities and educational institutions, the students are overwhelmingly from the place where these are situated. This makes them inward looking. It not only makes internationalization difficult, it is not good for the country itself. India is a country of diversities where plurality is a way of life. Educational institutions must reflect the diversity to foster cultural, linguistic, religious and regional acceptance. It will create a cohesive society. Further internal diversity is a stepping-stone to internationalization.

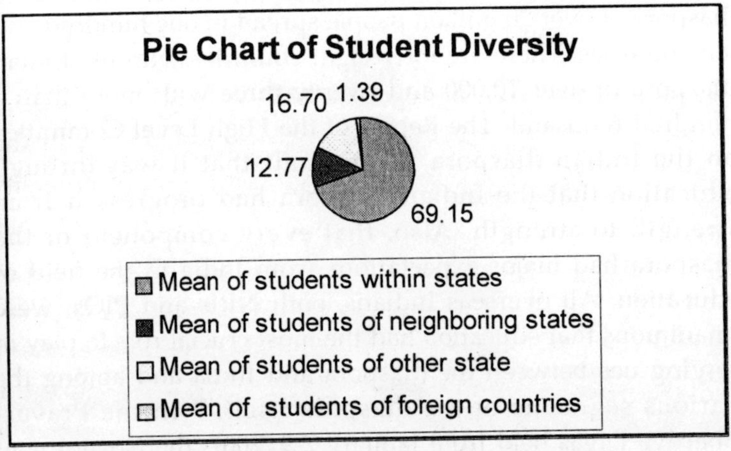
Pie Chart of Student Diversity
16.70
1.39
12.77
69.15
Mean of students within states
Mean of students of neighboring states
Mean of students of other state
Mean of students of foreign countries

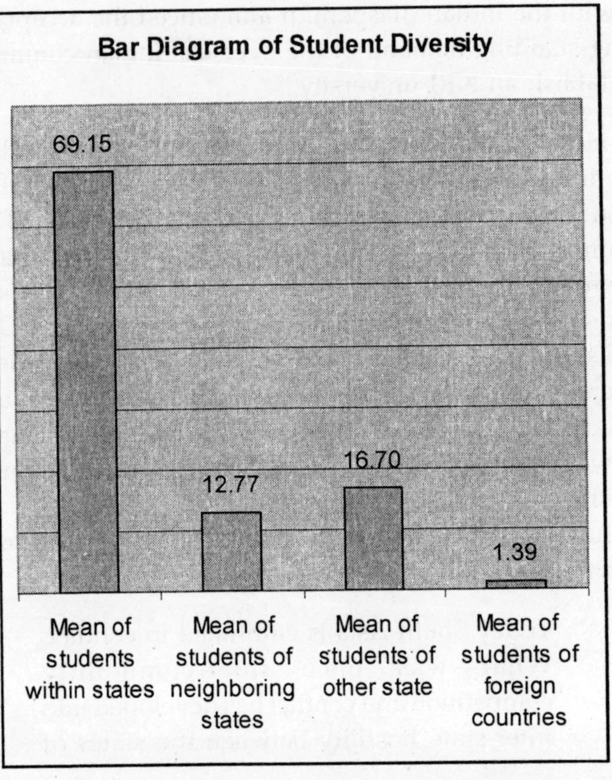
Bar Diagram of Student Diversity
69.15
12.77
16.70
1.39
Mean of students within states
Mean of students of neighboring states
Mean of students of other state
Mean of students of foreign countries

Moreover, it has to be remembered that India has a diaspora of over 20 million people spread in one hundred and ten countries. There are forty-eight countries with the Indian diaspora of over 10,000 and twenty-three with more than a hundred thousand. The Report of the High Level Committee on the Indian diaspora pointed out that it was through education that the Indian diaspora had progressed from strength to strength. Also, that every component of the diaspora had major expectations from India in the field of education. All overseas Indians, both NRIs and PIOs, were unanimous that education had the most crucial role to play in forging ties between the diaspora and India and among the various segments of the diaspora itself.[105] In the Pravasi Bhartiya Divas held from January 7-9, 2007, the Government of India recognized the role of education in strengthening ties with the Indian diaspora. It announced the acceptance of a long-standing demand of the overseas Indian communities to establish an NRI university.[106]

How urgent is the need to develop cooperation through the education sector can be seen from the idea of the South Asian University that was advanced by Prime Minister Manmohan Singh at the SAARC Summit in Dhaka on November 12, 2005. He offered to host it in India but any other suitable venue was also acceptable to him. Prof. Gowher Rizvi's draft of the concept and outline of the plan envisages a university that would provide the highest quality of education to students of South Asia.[107] This is seen as an imperative for the twenty-first century which will be the age of Knowledge Societies. However, apart from academic excellence, Rizvi has emphasized another of its dimensions of fundamental importance.

> Today South Asia is embroiled in conflict. What was once inter-community competition and conflict has developed into inter-state hostility between the states of

the region. While the neighbouring countries of Southeast Asia have prospered through cooperation, we in South Asia have remained mired in conflict, wasteful wars and a persistent attempt to 'beggar our neighbours'. The experience of the first half of the century since independence has been described as wasted years. Despite tremendous success in many areas and extraordinary individual achievements of the people of South Asia, the region remains mired in poverty; it is the home of half of the destitute and illiterates in the world today; it has gained the dubious distinction of being low down in most human development indicators; and is fast becoming a breeding ground for religious extremism and intolerance.

Our hopes that as the memories of Partition becomes distant, the hostilities and hatreds would diminish has sadly not happened. Hostilities and prejudices have passed from one generation to another with little sign of its abatement. This is easy to understand. There is very little contact between the young people of the region; they lack knowledge of each other; and in the absence of personal bonds and relationships (as the Partition generation had) their outlook is framed by hostile propaganda on all sides of the frontiers, biased educational curriculum, deep prejudices born out of ignorance of each other, and fears based on the

> 'demonization of the other'. If we want the future to be different from the past, we cannot do, nor have, more of the same. We will need to chart new visions and directions–build on a shared past to create a prosperous and peaceful future, a future based on cooperation and draw on common civilizational values. We remain so focused on conflicts and imagined differences that we forget our greatest assets that geography and a common past has bestowed on us. South Asia has advantages that other regions of the world can only dream of. It not only has a shared history, music, art and architecture, philosophy, literature and cuisine but also a syncretic culture and a common mode of discourse among its elite; and despite many years of division its economy remains largely integrated and has a linked system of transport (although temporarily disrupted). The University will be a major contribution towards rebuilding a shared future by providing a world class education to its future leaders and citizens.[108]

The High Level Committee, too, had made some crucial recommendations that need to be seriously considered and implemented. Apart from encouraging Diaspora Studies, it felt that Indian universities should institute India Study Programmes as had been done by the University of Hyderabad for both foreign students and for students from the Indian diaspora. In addition, there can be cultural youth exchange programme and internships with various organizations both in the public and the private sector in particular with Non-Governmental Organizations. A good model is the MASA (Journey) programme of Israel which is a partnership between the Government of Israel and the Jewish Agency both contributing US$ 50 million each. It enables students to spend a semester to a year in Israel travelling, studying and experiencing the culture at first hand.[109] The Ministry of Overseas Indians could look into the possibility of a similar programme.

Besides students, there are outstanding academics of Indian origin teaching in many universities abroad with expertise in various fields of technology, medicine, computers, engineering and others. Their help can be taken to conduct short-term courses or a series of lectures thereby forging links between Indian educational institutions and those abroad. Other measures can be in the field of distance education where IGNOU has already taken the lead and has established partnerships with centres in countries. These need to be further strengthened. More long-term initiatives are setting up of off shore campuses. A step has been taken by IIM Bangalore to establish a campus in Singapore. Universities of international standards can be set up in Export Promotion Zones which could be open to both Indian and international students. This could also stem the flow of Indian students seeking admission in foreign universities as full fee paying students. Currently India is the largest source country for students going to study in USA.

Conclusion

Therefore it is increasingly being accepted that one important role of education is bridge-building. It would be natural for India to take the lead in education. It can do so without it being a drain on its resources. Today India is a heavy importer of higher education. It has the potential to become its exporter. It would also enable it to strengthen its bonds with its diaspora and also help it to sustain its cultural and civilizational heritage. Members of the diaspora can not only make a contribution to the education sector in India, they are also important opinion makers in their host countries. They have developed India clubs and study groups in their own academic institutions that are of immense value in disseminating points of view and information pertaining to issues in India.

In today's world, if India wants to become a global player it must not only be a consumer of knowledge but also produce it. This was the vision of the Kothari Commission too. Indian education must contribute to the country's societal well-being and also provide leadership in knowledge generation. To do this, it must harness the academic talent that exists in the country and enlist the services of its educational institutions to create a world of ideas with intellectual leaders who create bonds between India and the world.

References

1. ICCR was envisaged by its founder President, Maulana Abul Kalam Azad, as an organization that would foster and strengthen cultural relations of India with the world. See http://www.iccrindia.org
2. Kothari Commission, (1964-1966) and its recommendations on education is a landmark in the history of education in India. The Education Commission of 1964-66, popularly known as the Kothari Commission, stressed that egalitarian and development goals in the country can best be achieved through education. It was envisaged that the national system of education would provide education to all students of comparable quality irrespective of caste, creed, location or sex. It was proposed that the government will initiate appropriately funded programmes and take effective measures towards the common school system. The purpose was to integrate the education system with socio-economic transformation and make it a vehicle of economic development. The task looked colossal needing a large quantity of financial resources.
3. *Ibid.*
4. See http://portal.unesco.org
5. Realism is an approach to the study and practice of international politics. It emphasizes the role of the nation-state and makes a broad assumption that all nation-states are motivated by national interests, or, at best, national interests disguised as moral concerns.
6. Hans J. Morgenthau, *Politics Among Nations. The Struggle for Power and Peace,* New York: Alfred A.Knopf, 1948.

7. Robert Keohane and Joseph Nye, *Transnational Relations and World Politics*, Cambridge: Harvard University Press, 1972.
8. Robert Keohane and Joseph Nye, *Power and Interdependence*, 2nd ed., Glenview, IL: Scott, Foresman, 1989.
9. Thomas Friedman, *The World is Flat: A Brief History of the Twenty-first Century*, New York: Farrar, Straus & Giroux, 2005
10. The democratic peace theory, liberal peace theory, or simply the democratic peace is a theory and related empirical research in international relations, political science, and philosophy which holds that democracies usually, liberal democracies—never or almost never go to war with one another. The original theory and research on wars has been followed by many similar theories and related research on the relationship between democracy and peace, including that lesser conflicts than wars are also rare between democracies, and that systematic violence is in general less common within democracies.
11. See http://portal.unesco.org
12. Thomas Friedman, *The World is Flat: A Brief History of the Twenty-first Century*, Farrar, Straus and Giroux, 2005. For Friedman, cheap, ubiquitous telecommunications have finally obliterated all impediments to international competition, and the dawning 'flat world' is a jungle pitting 'lions' and 'gazelles,' where 'economic stability is not going to be a feature' and 'the weak will fall farther behind.' Rugged, adaptable entrepreneurs, by contrast, will be empowered. The service sector telemarketing, accounting, computer programming, engineering and scientific research, etc., will be further outsourced to the English-spoken abroad; manufacturing, meanwhile, will continue to be off-shored to China. For Friedman, cheap, ubiquitous telecommunications have finally obliterated all impediments to international competition, and the dawning 'flat world' is a jungle pitting 'lions' and 'gazelles,' where 'economic stability is not going to be a feature' and 'the weak will fall farther behind.' Rugged,

adaptable entrepreneurs, by contrast, will be empowered. The service sector (telemarketing, accounting, computer programming, engineering and scientific research, etc.), will be further outsourced to the English-spoken abroad; manufacturing, meanwhile, will continue to be off-shored to China.

13. Utpal Bannerji,"Role of Cultural Diplomacy", *Indian Foreign Policy: Agenda for the 21st Century"*. Vol.I, ed., Lalit Mansingh *et al.* New Delhi: Foreign Service Institute and Konark Publishers, 1997, pp. 397-417.

14. Joseph Nye, *Power in the Global Information Age: From Realism to Globalization*, Routledge, 2004. See also Joseph Nye, Soft Power: The Means to Success in World Politics, New York: Public Affairs, 2004.

15. Joseph Nye, *Bound to Lead: The Changing Nature of American Power*, New York: Inc., Basic Books Inc., 1990 pp. 190-195. Joseph Nye, *The Paradox of American Power: Why the World's only Superpower Can't Go It Alone*, Oxford, New York: Oxford University Press, 2002.

16. Joseph Nye, *Bound to Lead*, pp. 190-195.

17. Steven Lukes, *Power: A Radical View*, London: Macmillan, 1974. Lukes' third dimension of power exists where people are subject to domination and acquiesce in that domination. The intentional stance allows us to predict and explain others' behaviour in ways that those agents may not recognize. It denies agents' privileged access to their own reasons for actions. Using the intentional stance, we can understand how agents may acquiesce in their own domination. We can also make distinctions between those who dominate knowingly and those who dominate without realizing they do so. It allows us to distinguish morally such cases and to understand the power structure without falling into the Foucaultian trap of seeing all social relationships in the same relativistic light and where all–dominant and dominated alike–are subject to the same power relations and moral responsibility.

18. *Ibid.*

19. *Ibid.*
20. Alvin Toffler, *Powershift: Knowledge, Wealth, and Violence at the Edge of the 21st Century,* New York, Toronto: Bantam Books, 1990, pp. 15-16.
21. *Ibid.*
22. *Ibid.*
23. Nye, *The Paradox of American Power: Why the World's Only Superpower Can't Go It Alone,* p.9.
24. In 2004, Nye analysed the concept even further and with greater urgency after the September 11 disaster in *Soft Power: The Means to Success in World Politics.*
25. *Ibid.*
26. Thomas Friedman, *The World is Flat: A Brief History of Twenty-First Century,* New York: Farrar Strauss and Giroux, 2005.
27. *Ibid.*
28. *Ibid.*
29. Utpal Bannerji, "Role in Cultural Diplomacy", *Indian Foreign Policy: Agenda for the 21st Century,* Vol. I, ed., Lalit Mansingh *et al.* New Delhi: Foreign Service Institute and Konark Publishers, 1997, pp. 397-417. See also, J.N. Dixit, "Culture as an Instrument of Diplomacy," *Indian Foreign Policy: Agenda for the 21st Century,* Vol. 1, pp. 418-428.
30. *Ibid.*
31. *Ibid.*
32. *Ibid.*
33. J.N. Dixit, *India's Foreign Policy 1947-2003,* New Delhi Picus 1998.
34. Amit Gupta, "India's Soft Power", *Indian Foreign Affairs Journal,* Vol. 1, No.1, January-March 2006, pp. 45-57.
35. *Ibid.*
36. *Ibid.*
37. Peter van Ham, "The Rise of the Brand State: the Postmodern Politics of Image and Reputation", *Foreign*

Affairs, September/October 2001, cited by Amit Gupta in "India's Soft Power".

38. Amit Gupta, "India's Soft Power".

39. Varun Sahani, "India as a Global Power: Capacity, Opportunity and Strategy", *Indian Foreign Policy: Agenda for the 21st Century*". pp. 21-41.

40. See www.mre.gov.br/cdbrasil/itamaraty/web/ingles/relext/mre/orgreg/mercom/index.htm-3k

41. Margaret Wyszomirski, "Negotiating the Global Maze Artfully, Going Global" Proceedings of the 2000 Bernett Arts and Public Policy Symposium, cited by Hawey B. Feigenbaum, "Globalization and Cultural Diplomacy," Centre For Arts and Culture Issue Paper, p.13. For Details see, www. gsfe.nasa.gov.

42. *Ibid.*

43. Thomas L. Friedman, *The Lexus and the Olive Tree,* New York: Farrar Strauss Giroux, 1999, pp. 7.

44. *Ibid.,* pp 7-8.

45. Thomas Friedman, *The World is Flat: A Brief History of the Twenty-First Century,* New York: Farrar Strauss and Giroux, 2005, p.356.

46. Hawey B. Feigenbaum, "Globalization and Cultural Diplomacy", Centre for Arts and Culture Issue Paper". For details see www.gsfc.nasa.gov

47. *Ibid.*

48. Shalini Veuturelli, "From the Information Economy to the Creative Economy: Moving Culture to the Centre of International Public Policy", paper prepared for the Centre for Arts and culture. Also cited by Hawey B. Feigenbaum.

49. *Ibid.*

50. William Glade, "Art, Culture, and the National Agenda," paper prepared for the Centre For Arts and Culture, cited by Hawey B. Feigenbaum, pp. 25-26.

51. Feigenbaum, p.27.

52. Richard Arndt, "Cultural Diplomacy and the Public Agenda," paper prepared for the Centre for the Arts and Culture, cited by Feigenbaum, p. 27.
53. William Glade cited by Hawey B. Feigenbaum, p. 28.
54. *Ibid.*, pp. 27-28.
55. Glade, cited by Feigenbaum, pp. 29-30.
56. Kevin Mulcahy, "Cultural Diplomacy in the Post-Cold War World," unpublished paper on file at the Centre For Arts and Culture, Washington, DC., 2000, cited by Feigenbaum, pp. 30-31.
57. See, www.nafsa.org
58. See, www.nsf.gov
59. *Ibid.*
60. David M. Reimers, *Still the Golden Door: The Third World Comes to America,* New York: Columbia University Press, 1985 p.99. See also, *Gale Encyclopedia of Multicultural America,* Vol.I, Detroit: Gale Research Inc., 1995, pp.125-126, pp.132-133. Irene Natividad and Susan B. Galls, ed., *Asian American Almanac*, U.X.L., An Imprint of Gale Research, 1996, pp.130-131. David Levinson, *Ethnic Groups Worldwide: A Ready Reference Handbook,* Arizona:The Oryx Press, 1998, p. 393.
61. *Ibid.*
62. A Common Faith: 40 years of Indo-US Cooperation, 1947-1987, USIS American Centre, New Delhi, 1987.
63. *Ibid.* See also M.V. Kamath, *The United States and India 1776-1996, The Bridge Over the River Time*, pp. 269-329.

    Asian American Almanac (1996), pp. 5-7.

    Joseph W. Elder, Edward C. Dimock, Jr., Ainslie T. Embree, ed., India's Worlds and US Scholars 1947-1997. pp. 27-37. See also, US Economic Assistance to India: An Overview and Highlights of the Past and Current Programmes, USAID India Programme Office, July 1993, pp.4-6, 9-10.

64. Lavina Malwani, "Indian Americans Finally Arrive in the American Political Process," http://www.littleindia.com/india/oct.2k/showtime.htm,p.3. For an overview of Indian Americans see "Indian American Community-A Story of Achievements", http://www.indianembassy.org/indusrel/comm.htm

65. Lavina Malwani, "Indian Americans Finally Arrive in the American Political Process", pp.3-5.

66. *Ibid.*

67. Maulana Azad in his inaugural address available at http://www.iccrindia.org

68. Ibid

69. Jawaharlal Nehru's inaugural address see http://www.iccrindia.org

70. *Ibid.*

71. *Ibid.*

72. Indian Technical and Economic Cooperation programme popularly known as "ITEC" was launched in 1964 as a bilateral programme of assistance of the Government of India. Under ITEC and its corollary SCAAP (Special Commonwealth Assistance for Africa Programme), 156 countries in Asia, East Europe, Central Asia, Africa and Latin America are invited to share in the Indian developmental experience acquired over five decades of India's existence as a free nation. ITEC is about cooperation and partnership for mutual benefit. It is response-oriented and it addresses the needs of developing countries. see http://itec.nic.in

73. *Ibid.*

74. The National University of Educational Planning and Administration (NUEPA), established by the Ministry of Human Resource Development, Government of India, is a premier organization dealing with capacity building and research in planning and management of education not only in India but also in South Asia. In recognition of the pioneering work done by the organization in the field

of educational planning and administration, the Government of India have empowered it to award its own degrees by way of conferring it the status of Deemed to be University in August, 2006) see http://www.nuepa.org. See Report of the Conference on Internationalization of Higher Education: Issues and Concerns, held on August 26-27, 2004, New Delhi: NIEPA, 2004.

75. see www.aiuweb.org. See also, K.B. Powar ed., Internationalization of Indian Higher Education: Papers presented at the Roundtable on "Internationalization of Indian Higher Education," organized by the Association of Indian Universities at the University of Mysore, Mysore on February 26-28, 2001.

76. The University Grants Commission has identified several countries for targeting to attract international students to India. Based on country profiles (demographic and economic) and taking into consideration, the present state of their Higher Education and Training System, skill gaps, programme for offer need to be identified. After this, issues like academic calendar, equivalence and matters relating to curriculum/language skills / maths skills / subject combination, etc. sorted out. There is a need to create a file on what is being offered and what is sought. see http://www.ugc.ac.in/new_initiatives/Preface.html

77. *Ibid.*

78. *Ibid.*

79. *Ibid.*

80. *Ibid.*

81. COPIE was a committee of the UGC under the PIHEAD programme

82. *Ibid.*

83. The National Assessment and Accreditation Council (NAAC) is an autonomous body established by the University Grants Commission (UGC) of India to assess and accredit institutions of higher education in the country. It is an outcome of the recommendations of the

National Policy in Education (1986) that laid special emphasis on upholding the quality of higher education in India. See www.naacindia.org

84. Pawan Agarwal (Unpublished Paper), "Higher Education Services in India and Trade Liberalization",

    See also, K.B. Powar, Sudhakar Pandey, Santosh Panda, Veena Bhalla, *International Students in Indian Universities*, New Delhi: Association of Indian Universities, 1997.

85. Pawan Agarwal, "Higher Education Services in India".

86. K.B. Powar, "Internationalization of Higher Education: Student Mobility, Institutional Links, Marketing and Government Policy," K.B. Powar ed., *Internationalization of Higher Education*, 2002, rpt. 2006. Pawan Agarwal, "Higher Education Services in India".

    See also, K.B. Powar, *Internationalization of Higher Education: Papers presented at the Roundtable on "Internationalization of Higher Education,"* organized by the Association of Indian Universities in association with and at Guru Nanak Dev University on February 25-27, 2002. New Delhi: Association of Indian Universities, 2002, rpt. 2006, pp.145-157.

87. Dubai Knowledge Village is located in the Dubai Technology and Media Free Zone near Dubai Internet City and Dubai Media City. By operating closely with its affiliate entities, Dubai Knowledge Village offers its partners a huge opportunity to collaborate with the business community to create a modern, vibrant learning environment.

88. Antony Bohm, "Growth in Demand for International Education by Students Worldwide, "Report of IDP Education Australia, 2003 cited by Pawan Agarwal "Higher Education Services in India".

89. See Powar, K.B. and Veena Bhalla (2001), "International Providers of Higher Education in India", International Higher Education, Centre for International Higher Education, Boston College, Spring 2001.

90. This was based on Pawan Agarwal combining the data for 82 Universities collected by the Association of Indian Universities for the year 2003-2004 with the projected data from 83 universities collected by the UGC in 2005 for the year 2001-2002. Out of 308 Universities that existed in 2003-2004, 109 universities reported no international students and 34 universities did not respond.
91. Pawan Agarwal, "Higher Education Services in India".
92. *Ibid*
93. Open Doors Report 2006. see opendoors.iienetwork.org
94. Veena Bhalla and Powar's research finds corroboration in Agarwal's study.
95. Powar, K.B. and Veena Bhalla, "International Providers of Higher Education in India", *International Higher Education*, Spring, 2001 Centre for International Higher Education, Boston College.
96. Data collected from a survey conducted for this paper.
97. *National Knowledge Commission Report*, Government of India, 2006. The National Knowledge Commission is a high-level advisory body to the Prime Minister of India, with the objective of transforming India into a knowledge society. It covers sectors ranging from education to e-governance in the five focus areas of the knowledge paradigm, such as: access, concepts, creation, applications and services.
98. Survey done by Pawan Agarwal on the geographical diversity of students in India on University campuses (Unpublished).
99. Cited in Larsen *et al.* "Trade in Educational Services: Trends and Emerging Issues", OECD Working Paper, OECD, Paris, 2002.
100. See Open Doors Report, opendoors.iienetwork.org
101. C. Jayanthi, "India's Groves of Academe Enriched," *The Indian Express*, December 6, 2006.

     See also, Arun Shourie, "Learning to Shield Our Excellence, "*The Indian Express*, March 24, 2007.

102. President Hamid Karzai. The impact of his educational experience in India was visible in the affection with which he remembered his teachers at the Himachal Pradesh University in Shimla from where he did his post graduation in Political Science. See http:// www.hindu. com/2006/11/16/ stories/2006111616414 00.htm

103. Nguyen Dy Nien's speech at Banaras Hindu University.

104. UGC has initiated the Study Abroad Programme. For details see www.ugc.ac.in

105. *Report of the High Level Committee on the Indian Diaspora*, New Delhi: Indian Council of World Affairs, 2001, pp. 439-457.

106. *Pravasi Bharatiya: Connecting India with Its Diaspora*, February 2007, Vol.2, No.2, Ministry of Overseas Affairs, p.7.

107. Prof. Gowher Rizvi's Penultimate Draft on South Asian University, October 27, 2006.

108. *Ibid.*

109. MASA, is the Gateway to Long-term Israel Programmes, which enables thousands of Jewish young adults to spend a semester to a year in Israel in over 150 approved programmes by providing information, contacts, grants and more. MASA's aim is to help young Jews to build a lasting relationship with Israel, its people and with other young Jews from all over the world, and to develop the tools they need to succeed in the coming years. Since its inception in 2004, MASA has established solid relationships with over 150 long-term Israel programmes, helping them to raise their level of accountability and quality of service to participants. see http://www.mas aisrael.org.

Select Reading

Books

1. *A Common Faith: 40 Years of Indo-US Cooperation, 1947-1987,* USIS American Centre, New Delhi, 1987.
2. Dixit, J.N., *India's Foreign Policy 1947-2003,* Picus: New Delhi, 1998.
3. Elder, Joseph W., Edward C. Dimock Jr., Ainslie T. Embree, ed., *India's Worlds and US Scholars 1947-1997,* New Delhi: AIIS/Manohar, 1998.
4. Friedman, Thomas J., *The Lexus and the Olive Tree,* New York: Farrar, Straus and Giroux, 2005.
5. Friedman, Thomas, *The World is Flat: A Brief History of the Twenty-first Century,* New York: Farrar, Straus and Giroux, 2005.
6. *Gale Encyclopedia of Multicultural America,* Vol. I, Detroit Gale Research Inc., 1995.
7. Kamath, M.V., *The United States and India 1776-1996 : The Bridge Over Time,* New Delhi: ICCR, 1998.
8. Keohane, Robert and Joseph Nye, *Power and Interdependence,* 2nd ed., Glenview: Scott Forseman, 1989.
9. Keohane, Robert and Joseph Nye, *Transnational Relations and World Politics,* Cambridge: Harvard University Press, 1972.
10. Lennon, Alexander T.J., ed., *The Battle for Hearts and Minds: Using Soft Power to Undermine Terrorist Networks,* Cambridge, Massachusetts; London, England: The MIT Press, 2003.

11. Levinson, David, *Ethnic Groups Worldwide: A Ready Reference Handbook,* Arizona: The Oryx Press, 1998.
12. Lukes, Steven, *Power: A Radical View,* London: Macmillan, 1974.
13. Mansingh, Lalit *et al., Indian Foreign Policy: Agenda for the 21st Century,* 2 Vols. New Delhi: Foreign Service Institute and Konark Publishers, 1997.
14. Morgenthau, Hans J., *Politics Among Nations: The Struggle for Power and Peace,* New York: Alfred A. Knopf, 1948.
15. UXL Natividad, Irene and Susan B. Galls, ed., *Asian American Almanac,* An Imprint of Gale Research, 1996.
16. Nye, Joseph, *Power in the Global Information Age: From Realism to Globalization,* Routledge, 2004.
17. Nye, Joseph, *Bound to Lead: The Changing Nature of American Power,* New York: Basic Books Inc., 1990.
18. Nye, Joseph, *Soft Power: The Means to Success in World Politics,* New York: Public Affairs, 2004.
19. Nye, Joseph, *The Paradox of American Power:*
20. Powar, K.B. ed., *Internationalization of Higher Education: Papers Presented at the Roundtable on 'Internationalization of Higher Education,'* organized by the Association of Indian Universities at the University of Mysore on February 26-28., 2001, New Delhi: Association of Indian Universities, 2001, rpt. 2006.
21. Powar, K.B., Sudhakar Pandey,Santosh Panda, Veena Bhalla, *International Students in Indian Universities,* New Delhi: Association of Indian Universities, 1997.
22. Powar, K.B. ed., *Internationalization of Higher Education: Papers Presented at the Roundtable on 'Internationalization of Higher Education,'* organized by the Association of Indian Universities in association with and at Gur Nanak Dev University of February 25-27, 2002, New Delhi: Association of Indian Universities, 2002, rpt., 2006.
23. Reimers, David M., *Still the Golden Door: Third World Comes to America,* New York: Columbia University Press, 1985.

24. Toffler, Alvin, *Powershift: Knowledge, Wealth and Violence at the Edge of the 21st. Century*, New York, Toronto: Bantam Books, 1990.

Reports and Articles

1. Agarwal, Pawan, "Higher Eduction Services in India and Trade Liberation," (Unpublished Paper).
2. Feigenbaum, Hawey B., "Globalization and Cultural Diplomacy," Centre For Arts and Culture Issue Paper, www. gsfc.nasa.gov.
3. Gupta, Amit, "India's Soft Power," *Indian Foreign Affairs Journal*, Vol. 1, No.1, January-March 2006.
4. Jayanthi., C. "India's Groves of Academe Enriched, "*The Indian Express*, December 2006.
5. Larsen *et al.*, " Trade in Educational Services:Trends and Emerging Issues", OECD Working Paper, OECD, Paris, 2002.
6. *National Knowledge Commssion Report*, Government of India, 2006.
7. Powar, K.B. and Veena Bhalla, "International Providers of Higher Education in India," *International Higher Education*, Centre for International Higher Education, Boston College, Spring 2001.
8. *Pravasi Bhartiya: Connecting India with Its Diaspora*, February 2007, Vol.2, No.2., Ministry of Overseas Affairs.
9. *Report of the High Level Committee on the Indian Diaspora*, New Delhi: Indian Council of World Affaris, 2001, pp.439-457.
10. Rizvi., Gowher, Penultimate Draft on South Asian University, October 27, 2006. (Unpublished).
11. Shourie, Arun, "Learning to Shield Our Excellence, "*The Indian Express*, March 24. 2007.
12. Venturelli, Shalini, "From the Informaiton Economy to the Creative Economy: Moving Culture to the Centre of

Internaitonal Public Policy". Paper prepared for the Centre for Arts and Culture.

13. http://www.hindu.com/2006/11/16/stories/200611161641400.htm
14. http://www.iccrindia.org
15. http://portal.unesco.org
16. www.mre.gov.br/cdbrasil/itamaraty/web/relext/mre/orgreg/mercom/index.htm-3k.
17. www.nafsa.org
18. www.nsf.gov
19. http://www.ugc.ac.in/new_initiatives/Preface.html
20. http://www.masaisrael.org.
21. http://www.littleindia.com/india/Oct.2k/showtime.htm
22. http://www.indianembassy.org/indusrel/comm.htm
23. Opendoors: iienetwork.org.

Appendix I

ADDRESS
By H.E. FOREIGN MINISTER NGUYEN DY NIEN
At the Banaras Hindu University

Prof. Dr. Shri Y.C. Simhadri, Vice-Chancellor
Distinguished guests
Ladies and Gentlemen

A Vietnamese proverb says: "Trees have roots, man has origins". As a Vietnamese, born and grown up in Vietnam, I devote all my life to the service of my country. However, it is still fresh in my mind the fond memories of the days I was in India forty years ago. What I absorbed and got enlightened during that time has become a source of my knowledge, which has greatly helped formulate my personality. Since then, even though I have had several opportunities to revisit India, I could not arrange to stay on as long as that previous time. Though many years have elapsed, my passions and feelings towards India live on afresh in my heart. To me, every visit to India seems to bring me back to a very close and dear place which is my second home.

It is therefore a special privilege for me to be conferred with the Honourable Doctorate, a noble scientific title under the unanimous decision by the Scientific Council of the Banaras

Hindu University, one of India's most prestigious and famous university. This time, I am on a pilgrimage to the older days and places of mine here and see the people that had made considerable contributions to my knowledge.

When I came here 40 years ago, this country was like an Egyptian Sphinx's puzzle to me. It was a fresh world that aroused my curiosity and passion. It was also a world filled with mysteries that were hard to fathom. I learnt Hindi. I bathed in the holy water of the Ganges. I chatted and became acquainted with Indian friends, and travelled to almost every state to discover India. I managed to get into the world of Premchand and Tagore's poetry and literature and traced back the Indian history through Nehru's writings. I read Gandhi's work to learn about Ahimsa, studied Radhakrishnan's works to understand a little bit about Indian philosophy and found out the links between India and Vietnam. India's culture, history, religions and philosophy were so appealing and interesting to me, I led a life as a real Indian in a diverse and distinctive culture, which is home to one of the brightest civilizations of mankind. Later on whenever I am in Vietnam or elsewhere in the world, those days continue to serve as a link between India and myself. Today, I return here with these feelings.

I am fortunate to have lived in a land of a brillant civilization and studied in such a famous university where got education from devoted teachers as well as assistance and sympathy from Indian friends. The honour I have today is therefore also attributed to the assistance extended by Indian teachers and friends to whom I am always grateful. As a Vietnamese proverb says, "No teachers, never success." would like to express today the most sincere sentiments to my Indian teachers and friends.

Ladies and Gentlemen, Vietnam and India have many historical and cultural similarities. The two countries have for a long time, entertained people-to-people contacts as well as economic, trade and religious links. The Nobel laureate Tagore came to Vietnam and the great man of culture Ho Chi Minh also visited India. Cultural interaction and the two countries' struggles for national liberation have brought Vietnam and India close to each other, augmenting into a lasting and noble friendship cultivated and fostered by our late leaders Jawaharlal Nehru and Ho Chi Minh. India and her people have always been with Vietnam even in times of the most severe hardships and difficulties on our path towards freedom, independence, national reunification and socialism. I am very proud of what I have contributed, although in a very small way, in my different capacities to the deepening of this friendship. India, on the other hand, has also greatly impressed upon Vietnam's modern diplomacy. One of my predecessors, an outstanding diplomat of Vietnam, the late Deputy Prime Minister and Foreign Minister Nguyen Co Thach, began his career in India as the first diplomatic representative of the new Vietnam in this subcontinent.

Our bilateral relations of friendship and cooperation have continued to consolidate and develop. Historical and cultural similarities and the common goal for national liberation have made Vietnam and India friends and reliable partners in our national economic development as well as regional and international integration. What we have scored is remarkable and important. And a brighter future is still ahead of us.

Ladies and Gentlemen, Indian history is unique. Rarely on our planet are there countries like India where exists religious and ethnic unity in diversity. In this connection, the Vedas have an important role to play. And all these together with peaceful character constitute the Indian identity. Unity in diversity is also the fundamental principle of ASEAN. This similarity alone indicates the firm foundations and bright future of the relations of friendship and cooperation between India and ASEAN as well as between India and each ASEAN Member Country. In this connection, the dialogue partnership between India and ASEAN is a necessity. Recently, the relations between

Member Country. In this connection, the dialogue partnership between India and ASEAN is a necessity. Recently, the relations between India and ASEAN have been given a new impetus by the launch of the Mekong-Ganga Cooperation, which has been put in concrete terms by the Hanboi Plan of Action and Cooperation projects adopted at the Second Mekong-Ganga Cooperation Ministerial Meeting in Hanoi last July.

India is gradually rising to the position of a Great Power, which is in consonance with her potential in natural and human resources, her time-honoured historical and cultural traditions. This is also in keeping with the expectations of her partners within and outside the region, including Vietnam.

Having travelled throughout Vietnam, I was amazed by many cultural and religious relics of Indian origin. I came to understand that thousands of years ago, our ancestors had already had close cultural links with the great Indian culture. My classmate, the late Dr. Cao Huy Dinh, received the Ho Chi Minh Award for his research project on Indian culture. In this regard, I understand that the Doctorate conferred on me today in my old school is a great honour not only for me, but for all Vietnamese who have studied in India and engaged in Indian studies. This is also a special manifestation of the friendship and cooperation between our two countries. Many among thousands of graduate and postgraduate students who had been trained in India have been in key positions in many scientific and socio-economic sectors of Vietnam at present. Just like me, they have become envoys, serving as a bridge spanning the two countries and the two peoples. In Vietnam, a growing number of people of all ages, sexes and social segments are interested in and eager to learn about India. Thus, it was not surprising that as many as 50,000 Vietnamese people have participated in the competition of Quiz on India launched by the Indian Embassy in Hanoi, Vietnam early this year on the occasion of the official friendship visit to Vietnam by H.E. Prime Minister Atal Bihari Vajpayee.

Ladies and Gentlemen, A Vietnamese saying goes, "He who teaches even a word becomes a teacher". Indian professors and friends taught me many things during my study at this university. Today, they honoured me with the Honorary Doctorate. Therefore, I would like to once again express my sincere and heartfelt thanks to Shri Y.C. Shimhadri, Vice-Chancellor, Members of the Scientific Council and all teachers of our university. I assure you that I will do my best to help further the Vietnam-India friendship, worthy of this prestigious Doctorate conferred to me, a student of the Banaras Hindu University.

In his famous work *The Discovery of India,* Jawaharlal Nehru wrote: "Life is a principle of growth, not of standing still, a continuous becoming, which does not permit static conditions." This reminds me that I should continue to study about India and explore the vast world of wisdom of the Indian people. I am confident I will be able to do so, let me quote Pandit Nehru again, ".....there is much in her that instinctively thrilled me".

The great land of India and the Banaras Hindu University will always be fresh in my mind and deep in my heart.

Appendix II

India-Africa Relations

ADDRESS

By His Excellency Dr. Bingu WA Mutharika
President of the Republic of Malawi
The State House LILONGWE MALAWI (AFRICA)

The Government of India, through the Indian Council for Cultural Relations (ICCR) has since the 1950s been providing education assistance to a number of African countries to study in India. As a result many students had an opportunity to obtain scholarships to acquire higher and better education that would not have been available to them.

I recall that the University of Delhi, alongside other universities throughout India had students from countries like Gold Coast (Ghana), Uganda, Northern Rhodesia (Zambia), Kenya, Southern Rhodesia (Zimbabwe), Nyasaland (Malawi), Sudan, Tanganyika (Tanzania), Ethiopia and Nigeria.

Most of the graduates of Indian Universities did rise to higher positions of responsibility and leadership in both public and private sector. These include personalities such as the late Dr. Daniel Lisulo of Zambia and Mr. Kintu Musoke of Uganda who served as Prime Ministers in their respective countries; Mr. Charles Nyereyegona who rose to the position of Chief

Executive of Lever Brothers (now Unilever)) in Southern Rhodesia just to mention a few.

As a result of the education I obtained in India, I am now the Head of State and Government of the Republic of Malawi. Prior to this I served as a distinguished international diplomat in the United Nations, the World Bank and the Common Market for Eastern and Southern Africa (COMESA).

Through education, India has made tremendous contribution of Africa's development including in areas of Science and Technology. Africa is also benefiting from the Indian breakthrough in a number of researches and developments that Africa requires, including agro-processing, industrial manufacturing, textiles, medical sciences, education, handicrafts and agricultural development.

His Excellency Dr. Bingu Wa Mutharika
President of the Republic of Malawi
The State House
Lilongwe
Malawi (Africa)

Appendix III
Your Educational Experience in India (Current Students)

Name:

Postal Address:

E-mail Address:

Nationality:

Institution in which you are enrolled:

Course Pursued:

Period of Study:

1. Your study is financed/sponsored by

   (a) Home Government/Home Institutions

   (b) Indian Government/Institutions

   (c) Self-financing

2. How did you obtain information about Indian institutions?

3. How did you decide on your present educational institution?

4. How did you decide on your course of study?

5. Did you have a preference for a particular city/town in India? If yes, the reasons for it.

6. Where do you stay ? In a hostel or an independent accommodation?

7. What were your experiences in the first week of your arrival?

8. How long did you take to settle down physically in India?

9. How long did you take to feel at home?

10. What is the nature of your peer group interaction?

11. Are you satisfied with the course that you are pursuing? How useful would it be on your return?

12. How would you compare the course that you are pursuing with similar courses in your country (especially in terms of cost, curriculum structure and professional management) ?

13. Would you have preferred pursuing some other course instead of the current one? If so, which course and why?

14. What have been your major professional experiences as a student in India?

15. What have been the major professional and personal impacts on you during your stay in India?

16. Please highlight some of the important incidents or events during your stay that stand out in your memory?

17. Would you recommend others to pursue a professional course in India? If yes, why ?

18. If no, what are the reasons?

19. Your suggestions to the institutions for improving/ reorienting the professional management of the courses being offered by them (specially in relation to the foreign students).

20. Does Education/Study abroad play a role in promoting relations between the countries? If so, how?

(a) Political (b) Economic and Commercial

(c) Cultural (d) Scientific and Professional domain

(e) Others

21. Your suggestions for promoting cooperation in the field of education between India and your country.

Note : Question numbers 1-13, 17 and 20 have been tabulated in Appendix IV

Weightage : Scaling has been done on a 5-point scale to evaluate the questionnaire for trends.

5 Strongly Agree

4 Agree

3 Disagree

2 Strongly Disagree

1 None of these.

*** The numbers in the Head Column of Appendix IV refer to the following questions :**

1 Your study is financed/sponsored by

(a) Home Government/Home institution

(b) Indian Government/Institution

(c) Self financing

2 How did you obtain information about Indian institution?

3 How did you decide on your present educational institution?

4 How did you decide on your course of study?

5 Did you have a preference for a particular city / town in India? If yes, the reason for it.

6 Where do you stay? In a hostel or an independent accommodation?

7 What were your experiences in the first week of your arrival?

8 How long did you take to settle down physically in India?

9 How long did you take feel at home?

10 What is the nature of your peer gorup interaction?

11 Are you satisfied with the course that you are pursuing? How useful it would be on your return?

12 How would you compare the courses that you are pursuing with similar courses in your country? (especially in term of cost, curriculum structure and professional management).

13 Would have preferred pursuing some other cours instead of the current one? If so which course anc why?

17 Would you recommend others to pursue professional course in India? If yes why?

20 Does education/study abroad play a role ir promoting relations between the countries? If yes

(a) Political (b) Economic

(c) Cultural (d) Scientific and professinal domain

(e) Others

Appendix IV

Study of Foreign Students in India (Current)

Sr. No.	Name	Country	Students	University	Sl. No. of Questions 1	2	3	4	5	6	7	8	9	10	11	12	13	17	20
1.	Getansalie	Barbodian	1	CMR	2	3	4	5	4	4	3	1	2	2	3	5	3	4	1
2.	Vinit Vishal Lal	Fiji	1	DU	5	3	3	3	4	5	3	5	5	2	3	4	3	3	5
3.	Aizada Mamytova	Kyrgyz	1	DU	5	3	1	5	4	5	2	4	3	1	5	3	5	5	5
4.	Nentawe Moses Gofwen	Nigerian	1	DU	2	3	3	3	4	5	2	2	2	4	5	2	3	2	4
5.	Mouhamed Jama Mivile	Ojiboutian	1	Nizam	2	4	3	4	5	4	5	1	1	4	5	5	3	5	3
6.	Virginia Ioana Guta	Romanian	1	Bangalore	4	5	5	5	4	4	2	3	1	1	1	5	5	4	5
7.	Sumeta Saniella Zelia	Seychellois	1	CMR	5	5	5	4	5	4	2	2	3	3	4	1	3	5	3
8.	Poyyayil Nicole	Swiss	1	Mumbai	2	3	3	3	1	4	2	4	2	1	2	2	3	2	2
9.	Mohd. Maan Fadel	Syrian	1	JNU	3	4	3	4	4	5	3	4	3	3	5	3	5	2	2
10.	James Beeson	British	2	IIM	2	3	5	5	5	5	4	4	4	5	5	4	4	5	4
11.	Irene Zaal	Dutch	2	AIESEC	2	3	3	3	4	2	3	3	2	1	3	4	3	3	5
12.	Mensur Mohammed	Etitrean	2	Nizam	3	3	3	4	5	3	3	4	5	5	5	4	5	5	3
13.	Baranowska Rudolph	French	2	MSRMC	2	3	4	2	4	4	2	2	2	3	4	4	3	2	4
14.	Rachael Wandtlle	German	2	Pune	2	3	5	5	4	5	2	5	5	5	4	2	5	3	5
15.	Kuma Winfred Lordson	Ghanian	2	Anand College	5	5	3	2	5	4	5	5	5	4	5	3	5	4	5
16.	Yutaka Mafsuzaki	Japan	2	L & T Engineer	2	4	5	5	4	5	2	2	4	3	2	2	2	4	3
17.	Hasan Majed Alqawasmeh	Jordanian	2	Jodhpur	2	5	5	5	4	4	5	4	4	5	5	2	3	2	5
18.	Rosalia Nadafuda Fotodela	Namibian	2	BN Bahadur	5	5	5	4	5	4	5	5	5	5	5	5	3	5	1
19.	Said M. R. Kewedar	Palestinian	2	DLS	2	3	3	4	4	4	2	3	2	3	4	3	3	5	2

Contd.

Sr. No.	Name	Country	Students	University	1	2	3	4	5	6	7	8	9	10	11	12	13	17	20
20.	Sunatullo Kudrator	Tajikistan	2	BIMS	5	5	5	5	5	4	3	4	5	4	4	5	4	5	5
21.	Bakundana Mantin	Ugandan	2	Mysore	5	3	5	5	4	4	3	4	5	4	5	5	5	5	5
22.	Terrence Karamba	Zimbabwean	2	Patel University	4	1	3	5	4	5	3	2	2	2	2	2	3	5	5
23.	Preethi Reddy	Australian	3	MCODS	2	4	5	5	5	5	5	4	3	2	3	5	5	4	4
24.	Seyun Yeom	Korean	3	KMC	2	3	3	5	5	5	5	2	3	3	3	3	3	4	4
25.	Abdirizak Hassan Mohamed	Somalian	3	Nizam	2	4	5	4	4	4	5	4	5	1	5	5	4	5	4
26.	TanTida Yodhasmvtr	Thai	4	Patel University	5	4	3	5	4	5	5	2	2	4	1	3	5	3	3
27.	Vu Thi Phuong Mai	Vietnamese	4	BN Bahadur	5	5	2	2	1	4	3	4	2	1	3	2	4	1	5
28.	Rabia Juma Rabia Al-Sadi	Omani	5	Nizam	2	4	3	4	4	4	5	3	5	3	4	5	4	4	4
29.	Nawras	Syrian	5	BVDU	4	5	4	5	4	1	3	2	1	1	4	3	3	5	5
30.	Jyoti Washden Nagarani	Indonesian	6	Manipal	2	3	4	4	4	5	4	5	5	4	4	5	4	5	4
31.	Basim A. Abood	Iraqi	6	—	2	1	1	4	5	4	2	2	5	1	3	5	5	1	2
32.	Sujan Das	Bangladeshi	7	—	5	5	3	5	4	5	1	5	2	2	2	3	1	3	5
33.	Odgeril Bumandalai	Mongolian	7	Patel University	5	3	3	5	4	5	2	4	2	1	3	5	5	5	2
34.	Ashin Pannashialankara	Myanmar	7	Pune	2	5	5	5	4	5	5	4	5	4	5	2	5	5	5
35.	Shani Abbas Kara	Canadian	8	MCODS	2	3	3	5	5	4	2	2	2	4	3	5	5	5	4
36.	Mhawila Ahmedi	Tanzanian	8	Fergusson	5	3	3	4	5	4	2	2	2	1	4	1	5	2	5
37.	Sardar Marinave	Uzbekistan	8	JNU	4	5	1	4	4	5	1	4	3	1	4	1	3	5	3
38.	Ali Abdal Mjeed Abdal	Sudanese	9	Manipal	3	3	4	4	4	3	4	4	5	4	5	5	5	5	4
39.	Ahmed Shareef	Maldivian	10	Mysore	5	5	4	4	4	4	2	4	4	5	3	5	4	5	4
40.	Emad Laud Abdulwahid	Yemeni	10	Patel University	5	5	5	5	4	4	2	2	2	2	2	3	5	2	5

Contd.

Sr. No.	Name	Country	Students	University	1	2	3	4	5	6	7	8	9	10	11	12	13	17	20
41.	Rafullah Hamedy	Afghan	11	Fergusson	5	5	5	5	4	4	2	2	2	1	4	3	3	3	5
42.	Adilah Inder Bibi	Mauritian	12	Manipal	2	3	4	5	4	5	4	2	2	4	4	5	3	5	5
43.	Bijal Shah	Kenyan	14	MAHE	2	3	3	5	5	5	4	5	5	5	4	5	5	5	5
44.	Saruhashini Maheswaran	Sri Lankan	14	MCODS	2	4	5	5	4	5	3	5	4	4	5	5	5	5	4
45.	Rachel Wirth	Etiopian	16	AIIS	4	4	4	4	4	4	3	4	4	4	5	4	5	5	5
46.	Phuntsho Gyattshen Dorgi	Bhutanese	21	GLC	2	3	4	5	4	5	1	4	2	3	5	5	3	5	3
47.	AP	American	22	AIIS	4	3	4	4	4	3	3	4	4	3	5	4	5	4	5
48.	Neeta Pradhan	Nepalese	22	Mumbai	2	5	5	4	4	4	5	4	5	5	5	4	3	1	4
49.	Mehna Nitin Chinchankar	NRI	36	IBB	2	3	5	5	4	5	5	5	5	4	3	4	5	4	1
50.	Majed Zamohmi	Iranian	38	Pune	2	3	4	5	4	4	2	4	4	4	4	4	5	2	5
51.	Rhema Sundram	Malaysian	51	KMC	4	3	3	5	5	5	3	2	2	1	5	2	2	5	4
52.	Md. Ilyas Noor	Afghan		DU	5	4	4	5	4	5	5	2	2	3	2	2	1	5	4
53.	Ajmal Zaki	Afghan		DU	2	3	5	5	5	5	1	2	2	1	5	1	5	3	4
54.	Shafiquallah Zaheer	Afghan		Osmania	5	4	5	4	4	5	4	4	3	4	3	5	4	5	4
55.	Obaidullah Burhari	Afghan		Osmania	5	5	2	5	1	4	2	1	1	1	5	5	5	5	4
56.	Md. Hanif Sufizoda	Afghan		Osmania	5	5	5	5	4	4	4	4	4	5	5	5	5	5	4
57.	Hunar Sanzar	Afghan		Osmania	5	4	4	5	4	4	4	4	2	3	5	5	5	5	5
58.	Amena Mohammadi	Afghan		Osmania	5	4	4	5	4	4	5	4	1	4	5	5	5	1	5
59.	Mariam Sayor	Afghan			5	4	5	2	4	5	5	3	4	5	4	5	5	5	5
60.	Ashna Obaidullah	Afghan		Pune	5	5	1	5	4	4	5	4	2	3	5	4	5	2	4

Contd.

Sr. No.	Name	Country	Students University	1	2	3	4	5	6	7	8	9	10	11	12	13	17	20
61.	Sayed Mohammed Saeq Shijjan	Afghan	Pune	5	5	5	1	1	5	2	5	2	1	3	3	5	5	5
62.	Isabelle Jennings	American	JNU	3	4	5	5	4	5	4	4	4	1	5	5	5	5	4
63.	Gary Philips	American	DU	2	3	5	5	5	5	1	2	3	1	1	1	5	3	4
64.	Rebecca Cowen	American	DU	2	3	5	3	4	5	2	3	5	3	3	5	3	2	4
65.	Gopala Konerl	American	KMC	2	3	3	5	5	3	4	5	4	3	5	5	4	5	3
66.	Sumana Reddy	American	KMC	2	3	5	5	5	5	5	5	3	1	4	3	5	5	3
67.	Thomas Lin	American	KMC	2	3	5	5	4	5	5	3	5	5	4	1	5	4	4
68.	Kavita K. Salvi	American	MCODS	2	3	5	5	4	5	2	3	5	5	5	5	5	5	5
69.	Tapasya Kher	American	MSRMC	2	4	4	3	5	3	5	5	5	5	5	2	4	5	4
70.	Arshad Khashaya John	American	MSRMC	2	5	2	3	4	2	2	2	2	3	5	2	4	2	2
71.	Dennis Mathew Koppuzha	American	MSRMC	2	3	4	4	3	5	3	3	2	2	5	5	5	5	3
72.	Amitoj Singh	American	Manipal	2	3	4	4	5	5	5	3	2	4	4	3	5	5	4
73.	M.	American	AIIS	4	3	3	3	4	3	4	3	4	3	4	4	4	4	5
74.	David Bod	American	AIIS	4	4	4	1	5	4	1	4	4	4	1	1	1	1	1
75.	Peter Nasuti	American	AIIS	4	4	4	5	5	3	4	5	5	5	4	5	5	5	5
76.		American	AIIS	4	4	5	5	4	5	3	4	3	3	4	5	5	5	5
77.	Shams-Tabraiz Muzaffar	American	AIIS	4	3	3	4	4	3	4	4	5	4	5	5	5	5	5
78.	Sadaf Jaffer	American	AIIS	4	4	4	4	4	4	5	4	5	5	5	5	5	3	5
79.	Daniel Maschroniz	American	AIIS	4	4	4	4	4	4	4	4	2	3	4	4	4	5	5
30.	Holly Donahue Singh	American	Lucknow	5	5	4	5	5	3	4	4	5	4	4	3	4	4	5

Contd.

Sr. No.	Name	Country	Students University	1	2	3	4	5	6	7	8	9	10	11	12	13	17	20
81.	Bridget Kustin	American		5	5	5	5	4	4	3	4	4	4	5	5	5	5	5
82.	Adam Brown	American	AIIS	5	4	4	4	4	3	4	4	4	4	5	5	5	5	5
83.	Rev Hien Nagujm	Australian	DU	2	3	3	5	4	5	2	2	1	2	4	3	5	3	1
84.	Vidya Jacob	Australian	KMC	2	3	5	5	5	5	3	3	5	5	5	2	5	4	3
85.	Jyoti Baral	Bangladeshi	CMR	5	4	5	5	4	5	5	4	4	5	5	4	3	5	4
86.	Priyoti Mandal	Bangladeshi	CMR	5	3	5	5	5	4	5	1	4	5	5	5	3	5	3
87.	Rajib Talukdar	Bangladeshi	CMR	2	3	1	4	5	4	5	2	2	1	5	4	3	4	2
88.	Narayan Biswas	Bangladeshi	CMR	5	5	5	5	4	4	3	1	2	3	3	4	1	4	3
89.	Angkita Guha	Bangladeshi	MIOT	2	3	3	3	4	5		3	5	4	4		3	5	2
90.	Intekhab Hussain	Bangladeshi	Manipal	2	5	3	3	5	4	4	5	5	4	4	5	3	5	4
91.	Gaki	Bhutanese	CMR	2	3	4	4	4	4	3	3	2	1	5	2	2	4	3
92.	Pemchoki	Bhutanese	CMR	2	3	3	4	5	4	2	3	4	5	5	5	3	5	3
93.	Yeshey Wangchuk	Bhutanese	CMR	2	3	4	5	1	5	2	3	4	1	5	5	4	2	5
94.	Karma	Bhutanese	CMR	2	3	3	5	1	4	4	3	3	1	3	3	5	5	2
95.	Pinchen Dema	Bhutanese	CMR	2	3	4	4	1	4	4	4	4	4	3	4	1	5	2
96.	Karma Yangzom	Bhutanese	CMR	2	3	1	4	4	5	4	2	4	5	2	2	2	5	1
97.	Chehi Zangmo	Bhutanese	CMR	2	3	5	4	4	4	3	3	2	5	5	5	4	5	3
98.	Thinlesy Yangzom	Bhutanese	CMR	2	3	4	4	4	4	3	4	2	5	5	2	3	5	4
99.	Lobzang Nima	Bhutanese	CMR	2	3	4	4	5	4	5	4	5	4	5	5	3	5	3
100.	Namgay Lham	Bhutanese	CMR	2	3	3	4	5	4	4	4	2	1	4	2	3	5	2

Contd.

Sr. No.	Name	Country	Students University	1	2	3	4	5	6	7	8	9	10	11	12	13	17	20
101.	Babul	Bhutanese	CMR	2	3	4	5	4	4	2	4	2	5	5	4	5	5	2
102.	Ashit Rai	Bhutanese	CMR	2	3	3	5	5	4	3	4	2	1	3	3	3	4	1
103.	Rigim Nidop	Bhutanese	CMR	2	3	4	4	4	4	4	2	2	4	5	2	2	4	2
104.	Tshering Dolkar	Bhutanese	CMR	2	3	3	5	5	4	3	3	2	5	5	2	3	5	4
105.	Alisha Mukhia	Bhutanese	CMR	2	3	4	5	5	4	2	3	2	5	5	4	3	5	4
106.	Kinley	Bhutanese	CMR	2	3	4	3	4	4	3	4	2	2	1	2	4	5	4
107.	Kinely Pekom	Bhutanese	CMR	2	3	4	5	4	4	1	3	2	3	3	2	3	5	1
108.	Navina Thapa	Bhutanese	CMR	2	3	3	2	4	4	2	2	2	4	5	4	5	4	3
109.	Tshering Choki	Bhutanese	CMR	2	3	4	4	4	4	3	3	3	1	4	5	3	5	3
110.	Tenzie Pelden	Bhutanese	CMR	2	3	3	5	4	4	3	3	2	1	5	4	3	5	3
111.	Jay Tuakea	Britisher	MCODS	2	3	3	5	5	5	4	2	3	4	4	3	5	5	3
112.	Gurpreet Singh Jaura	Canadian	Manipal	2	5	5	5	4	5	3	2	5	5	5	5	5	5	2
113.	Manjula Mahadeva	Canadian	KMC	2	4	1	5	4	5	1	3	2	3	1	5	3	3	3
114.	Priyadharshny S.	Canadian	KMC	2	3	5	5	5	5	2	3	3	5	3	2	5	3	4
115.	Kowthemi Murugapoopathy	Canadian	MCODS	2	3	3	5	5	5	4	5	5	5	4	5	5	5	5
116.	Zahid Jvma	Canadian	MCODS	3	3	5	5	5	5	2	2	2	3	3	2	5	5	5
117.	Gurpreet Singh Jaura	Canadian	MCODS	2	3	4	5	4	5	3	3	5	5	4	5	3	5	2
118.	Brian Rasquinha	Canadian	MCODS	2	3	3	3	5	5	2	5	5	3	1	3	1	1	1
119.	Karir Doornbos	Dutch	AIESEC	3	3	3	3	4	4	4	3	3	5	3	2	3	2	1
120.	Tesfaye Abera	Ethiopian	CIEFL	4	4	4	4	5	3	4	4	4	5	5	5	5	5	5

Contd.

Sr. No.	Name	Country	Students University	1	2	3	4	5	6	7	8	9	10	11	12	13	17	20
121.	Tesfaye Dagnew G.	Ethiopian	CIEFL	4	5	5	5	5	3	4	3	3	4	5	5	1	5	5
122.	Tadesse Boyossa	Ethiopian	CIEFL	4	5	5	4	5	1	3	4	3	3	5	4	4	5	5
123.	Abdi Nisir Seid Musse	Ethiopian	Nizam	3	3	5	5	5	3	3	3	4	3	4		4	5	4
124.	G.T. Enofshaw	Ethiopian	IDS	5	4	3	5	4	4	5	5	3	2	5	4	5	5	5
125.	Abdureshi D. Beshir Sehenter	Ethiopian	Nizam	2	3	4	4	4	4	1	4	4	4	5	5	4	4	2
126.	Yohannes	Ethiopian	Mysore	5	5	5	3	5	4	2	5	2	5	4	3	5	5	1
127.	Solomon Shewarega	Ethiopian	IDS	5	4	3	2	4	4	3	4	4	5	3	5	5	5	5
128.	Getachew M. Mabtemariom	Ethiopian	CS	5	3	4	3	5	5	5	5	5	5	3	3	3	5	5
129.	Sharif	Ethopian	Osmania	2	3	3	1	4	4	1	2	3	3	5	3	3	5	2
130.	Aboli Warsame Hirsi	Ethopian	Osmania	3	4	5	5	5	3	4	4	5	5	5	5	4	5	5
131.	Mohied Omer Husseiin	Ethopian	Osmania	3	4	5	5	5	3	3	4	3	3	1	1	3	5	1
132.	Ibrahim	Ethopian	Osmania	3	4	5	5	5	4	5	5	5	5	5	5	1	5	5
133.	Groum	Ethopian	PUV	2	5	5	5	1	5	2	2	2	2	2	2	5	3	3
134.	Faisel Mohammed Ismail	Ethopian		1	1	1	1	4	3	4	3	3	5	5	1	4	4	3
135.	Dahir Mohamed	Etiteria	Nizam	2	3	3	4	5	5	3	1	1	4	5	2	2	1	2
136.	Pednit Thomas	French	L. Tees	4	3	5	1	5	5	3	3	4	1	5	2	4	1	4
137.	Ktistina Stegner	German	AIESEC	2	3	3	3	4	4	3	5	2	3	5	1	2	5	5
138.	Willam Osei Sarpong	Ghanian	CMR	5	3	1	4	4	4	1	3	3	5	4	4	5	5	3
139.	Iskandar	Indonesian	JNU	3	5	5	5	5	5	3	4	4	5	5	5	5	1	1
140.	Fachim	Indonesian	JNU	4	5	5	5	5	5	3	3	3	2	5	5	5	5	4

Contd.

Sr. No.	Name	Country	Students University	1	2	3	4	5	6	7	8	9	10	11	12	13	17	20
141.	Ebiet Kurniawan	Indonesian	CIEFL	5	5	4	5	5	3	3	4	1	1	5	4	5	4	5
142.	Susanto	Indonesian	CIEFL	3	3	4	4	5	3	3	3	5	3	5	4	1	1	1
143.	Deri Sis Nanda	Indonesian	CIEFL	5	4	4	4	5	3	3	3	4	3	4	4	5	5	3
144.	Abbas Hashat Tehran	Iranian		2	1	1	1	1	4	3	1	1	1	5	3	1	4	5
145.	Md. Mahdi Sahromi	Iranian	IIT Delhi	2	4	4	5	4	5	2	5	5	3	1	4	5	5	4
146.	Ali Rahmani	Iranian	IIT Delhi	4	3	5	5	4	5	2	2	2	1	5	2	5	2	2
147.	Hossein Noferesh	Iranian	IIT Delhi	4	3	4	3	4	5	2	3	2	3	3	3	1	3	4
148.	Masoud Iranmanesh	Iranian	IIT Delhi	4	4	2	3	5	5	2	2	3	4	3	1	3	2	5
149.	Sahand Taba Tabaei	Iranian	CMR	2	3	3	5	4	4	2	2	2	3	3	4	3	1	5
150.	Woranal Lumbenmul	Iranian	CMR	2	3	1	5	5	4	4	3	2	1	1	4	1	1	4
151.	Hadi Shayeshteh	Iranian	CMR	2	3	4	3	4	4	2	2	2	3	3	5	2	2	5
152.	Seyed Farzad Jamalian	Iranian	KMC	2	3	5	5	4	4	2	2	2	1	4	3	5	5	3
153.	Mehdi Ostovan	Iranian	KMC	2	3	5	5	4	4	3	2	2	1	4	5	5	5	4
154.	Ghazal Sheikholeslahi	Iranian	Bangalore	2	3	5	5	4	4	4	2	3	1	1	1	1	2	5
155.	Hamid Reze Bouzegar	Iranian	Mysore	5	5	4	5	5	4	5	4	4	5	5	5	4	5	4
156.	Mohammad Reza	Iranian	VIT College	2	3	3	4	4	4	5	3	4	5	5	4	4	5	4
157.	Mahsa Maleks	Iranian	BN Bahadur	5	5	5	4	5	4	4	4	5	5	5	5	4	5	4
158.	Saeideh Saeidi	Iranian	BN Bahadur	5	5	5	5	4	4	4	4	5	3	5	5	4	5	5
159.	Md. Ali Moshrefi Zadeh	Iranian	YM College	2	3	5	5	4	4	2	2	2	4	5	4	4	5	5
160.	Yekta Yazdani	Iranian	KC College	2	3	3	3	4	5	4	5	2	1	5	4	5	5	5

Contd.

Sr. No.	Name	Country	Students University	1	2	3	4	5	6	7	8	9	10	11	12	13	17	20
161.	Mausa S. Kashani	Iranian	KC College	2	3	4	5	5	4	4	3	3	5	5	4	4	5	4
162.	Mohsen S. Kashani	Iranian	KC College	2	3	4	5	4	4	4	3	3	5	5	4	5	5	4
163.	Md. Sheikh Mohammadi Khamseh	Iranian	MIT	2	3	3	4	5	4	1	5	4	3	4	4	4	2	3
164.	Ferik Gharibian	Iranian	YM College	2	3	4	5	4	4	2	2	2	1	5	2	3	4	5
165.	Armin Amin Nejad	Iranian	YM College	2	3	5	5	4	4	3	4	3	1	5	5	4	5	5
166.	Marzick Tarahomi	Iranian	BVDU	2	3	4	1	4	4	5	5	4	4	5	4	5	2	5
167.	Fatemeh Khareghanian	Iranian	Pune	2	3	4	1	4	4	5	4	2	2	5	4	4	2	5
168.	Sareh Kheirabadi	Iranian	Fergusson	2	4	5	5	4	5	5	4	4	5	5	4	4	4	1
169.	Lossein	Iranian	Pune	2	3	3	4	5	4	2	2	2	1	2	2	2	2	4
170.	Nahid Shariki	Iranian	Fergusson	2	3	5	4	4	4	2	4	4	1	5	4	4	4	4
171.	Gholam Hussein Ahmadi	Iranian	Pune	2	3	4	4	4	4	5	4	5	5	5	5	5	4	5
172.	Uajed Zamohani	Iranian	Pune	2	3	4	5	4	4	2	4	4	4	4	4	5	2	
173.	Mohammad Peikari	Iranian	MIT	2	3	5	3	4	4	2	2	2	4	4	4	4	1	4
174.	Hamed Peikari	Iranian	MIT	2	5	5	4	5	4	2	2	2	1	4	2	3	5	5
175.	Kamran Janfeshan	Iranian	Pune	5	3	3	5	4	5	5	5	5	5	4	5	5	5	4
176.	Pooja Safari	Iranian		2	3	5	5	1	1	2	5	5	1	1	2	5	3	3
177.	Yasaman Shivani	Iranian	Fergusson	2	3	5	5	5	4	1	4	2	3	3	3	3	3	3
178.	Elahen Haghayegh	Iranian	Fergusson	2	5	5	5	4	4	2	2	2	3	3	3	5	2	4
179.	Kairash Kioahdoor	Iranian	Fergusson	2	3	1	5	5	4	2	2	5	1	3	3	5	2	3
180.	Kordi Tamandani Khaled	Iranian		2	3	4	4	4	4	1	2	2	3	3	3	2	1	1

Contd.

Sr. No.	Name	Country	Students University	1	2	3	4	5	6	7	8	9	10	11	12	13	17	20
181.	Lahib I. Z. AlSaaadi	Iraqi	Patel University	2	3	5	5	4	4	2	2	2	4	3	3	5	5	4
182.	Ahmed A.A.	Iraqi	Pune	5	3	5	5	4	5	2	5	4	5	5	5	5	2	5
183.	Ameer A.S. AlSwidi	Iraqi	Patel University	2	3	4	5	5	4	3	5	5	4	3	3	5	5	2
184.	Khalid W.Ali	Iraqi	Patel University	2	3	5	5	1	4	4	4	5	4	3	3	5	5	5
185.	Mohamme Mehar Hussain	Iraqi	Patel University	2	3	3	5	5	4	2	5	5	1	3	5	5	5	3
186.	Yumi Ashimiru	Japan	NGO	2	4	3	3	4	5	4	5	5	5	5	2	3	5	3
187.	Ghanem Saleh	Jordanian	MCL	2	3	5	5	5	5	2	3	5	5	3	3	5	5	3
188.		Kenyan		5	5	5	4	5	5	3	4	4	5	2	1	1	4	4
189.	Jigna Modha	Kenyan	Mangalore	2	3	5	5	5	5	5	2	3	4	5	2	5	5	4
190.	Zamzam Adan	Kenyan	DU	2	5	4	4	5	5	2	4	3	4	3	1	5	2	3
191.	Abdi Md. Ibrahim	Kenyan	DU	2	5	3	3	4	5	2	2	2	2	3	2	1	2	2
192.	Abdi M. Ah.	Kenyan	DU	4	5	5	5	4	5	2	2	5	5	4	5	3	5	4
193.	Lavenda Lisangari	Kenyan	DU	5	5	5	5	5	5	2	5	1	5	4	2	2	1	3
194.	Jouva Thure Odada	Kenyan	CMR	5	2	5	5	4	5	5	4	5	5	5	3	3	4	2
195.	Khilnna Shah	Kenyan	MCODS	2	3	3	5	5	5	2	2	2	5	3	5	5	5	2
196.	Sanaa Bhimsi	Kenyan	MCODS	2	3	1	1	5	4	5	2	2	5	3	4	5	5	2
197.	Cardine Johnson	Kenyan	MIT	2	3	3	3	5	5	2	5	5	5	5	5	5	1	4
198.	Jigna Modha	Kenyan	MCODS	2	3	4	5	5	5	4	2	2	4	3	2	5	5	4
199.	Veer Patel	Kenyan	Manipal	2	3	3	5	4	5	3	4	2	2	4	4	5	2	4
200.	Bariah Atemyo	Kenyan	IMED	2	5	5	5	4	4	5	4	2	2	5	2	4	3	1

Contd.

Sr. No.	Name	Country	Students University	1	2	3	4	5	6	7	8	9	10	11	12	13	17	20
201.	Min Hi Cho	Korean	CMR	5	4	4	3	5	4	1	5	5	1	3	1	3	2	3
202.	Yang Hyun Sesk	Korean	CMR	2	3	1	3	4	4	2	1	5	1	2	2	1	2	1
203.	Dhanya Panicker	Malaysian	Manipal	2	5	5	5	5	4	5	3	4	5	5	5	5	5	2
204.	Prisila Thandbalan	Malaysian	KMC	2	5	5	5	5	4	3	4	5	4	5	5	1	5	3
205.	Rajveer Singh Dhaliwal	Malaysian	Mangalore	2	3	3	3	4	5	3	4	5	5	5	5	1	5	3
206.	Vivegan Doraisamy	Malaysian	Mangalore	2	5	5	5	4	4	2	2	2	4	5	4	5	5	4
207.	Devarsin Krishnan	Malaysian	Manipal	2	4	5	5	5	4	3	3	5	5	5	5	5	5	1
208.	Jaunta Rajau	Malaysian	Mangalore	2	3	3	3	5	4	2	2	5	1	5	5	5	5	3
209.	Oot Earn Leong	Malaysian	KMC	2	5	3	3	5	5	5	5	5	4	5	5	3	5	3
210.	Gary Soon Pousiong	Malaysian	Manipal	2	3	5	5	1	4	2	5	2	4	3	3	5	5	2
211.	NG Ling Kang	Malaysian	Manipal	2	3	4	5	4	5	2	4	5	4	4	3	5	3	3
212.	Rajveer Singh Dhaliwal	Malaysian	Mangalore	2	3	3	3	4	5	5	3	5	3	3	5	3	5	3
213.	Krishna Al Shanmugam	Malaysian	RMC	2	3	3	3	4	4	5	3	4	4	4	1	3	4	4
214.	Norman O. David	Malaysian	RMC	2	3	3	5	4	4	4	2	2	4	2	3	5	4	4
215.	Adriana Siegang Langat	Malaysian	KMC	4	3	3	3	4	4	2	2	2	2	4	4	5	5	1
216.	V.M. Salvaksmori M	Malaysian	KMC	4	4	3	3	5	4	2	2	2	1	3	4	5	4	5
217.	Zulkarnain Bin Md. Noor	Malaysian	KMC	4	4	3	4	5	5	3	5	5	1	3	2	1	2	2
218.	Wilson Mathew Rong	Malaysian	KMC	4	4	3	4	5	5	2	5	5	3	3	2	5	2	2
219.	Ghantan Palanisamv	Malaysian	KMC	4	3	3	5	5	5	5	4	5	1	4	2	5	4	5
220.	Ong Hond Giap	Malaysian	KMC	2	3	1	5	1	5	2	4	5	1	5	2	5	4	3

Contd.

Sr. No.	Name	Country	Students University	1	2	3	4	5	6	7	8	9	10	11	12	13	17	20
221.	Gaddafi Bin Mostaffa	Malaysian	KMC	4	3	3	3	4	5	4	5	5	3	5	2	3	3	5
222.	Goh Jun Huj	Malaysian	KMC	4	3	3	3	5	4	2	3	5	1	3	4	5	4	2
223.	Andrew Ling Jing Seng	Malaysian	KMC	4	3	3	3	4	5	2	3	5	1	3	2	5	4	2
224.	Pang Jing Leek	Malaysian	KMC	2	2	2	5	5	5	2	3	2	3	1	5	3	3	2
225.	Ahbirami Pupramaniam	Malaysian	Manipal	2	4	4	5	4	5	4	5	4	4	5	5	5		4
226.	Gay Soon Pousiong	Malaysian	MAHE	2	3	4	5		4	2	4	2	4	3	3	3	4	2
227.	NG Ling Kang	Malaysian	MCODS	2	3	3	5	4	5	2	4	5	3	3	3	5	3	3
228.	Vivegan Doraisamy	Malaysian	MCODS	2	4	4	5	4	4	2	2	2	5	3	2	5	5	4
229.	Vidhya Lakshmi	Malaysian	MCODS	2	4	3	5	4	5	2	2	2	3	3	4	3	3	3
230.	Deviarsin Krishnan	Malaysian	MCODS	2	4	4	5	5	4	2	4	5	4	5	4	3	4	1
231.	Oot Ean Leong	Malaysian	KMC	2	5	5	3	5	5	5	5	5	3	4	4	5	5	3
232.	Vidhaya Lakshmi	Malaysian	MCODS	2	5	3	4	4	5	2	2	2	3	3	3	3	3	3
233.	Prisila Thanabalam	Malaysian	KMC	2	3	5	5	5	4	3	4	2	4	4	4	1	5	3
234.	Dhanya Panicker	Malaysian	Manipal	2	3	4	4	5	4	5	4	5	4	1	5	5	5	2
235.	Jaunta Raju	Malaysian	Manipal	2	3	3	3	5	4	3	2	4	1	4	4	3	5	3
236.	Teng Hong Ling	Malaysian	KMC	4	3	5	4	1	1	2	2	1	3	4	2	2	3	4
237.	Chong Siew Kounq	Malaysian	KMC	4	3	3	3	1	4	2	2	2	3	4	3	3	4	3
238.	Azuwairce Bin Amir	Malaysian	KMC	4	3	1	5	5	4	2	2	2	1	3	4	4	4	3
239.	Nur Khairiyah	Malaysian	KMC	4	3	3	5	4	4	2	2	2	1	5	2	2	3	5
240.	Haslin Azira Binti Mahmup	Malaysian	KMC	4	3	3	3	5	4	2	2	2	4	3	1	1	1	5

Sr. No.	Name	Country	Students University	1	2	3	4	5	6	7	8	9	10	11	12	13	17	20
241.	Noraelena Binti Abdullah	Malaysian	KMC	4	4	4	5	5	4	2	2	2	1	5	5	3	5	5
242.	Fatim Haziqah Bt. Matrebi	Malaysian	KMC	4	3	4	5	5	5	4	3	5	5	4	5	5	5	2
243.	Ch,NG Wan Ping	Malaysian	KMC	4	3	4	5	5	4	2	3	2	3	4	3	3	5	5
244.	Alifah Hasinah Binti Hassan	Malaysian	KMC	4	4	4	5	4	4	2	2	2	1	3	5	3	5	1
245.	Maizatul Aliaa Binti Abdul Manan	Malaysian	KMC	4	4	4	5	4	4	2	3	2	1	3	4	3	5	5
246.	Liu Chee Chang	Malaysian	KMC	4	4	3	5	5	5	2	2	2	3	3	2	2	4	5
247.	Nur Diyanah jabarullah	Malaysian	KMC	4	5	4	5	5	4	3	2	2	4	4	2	2	5	4
248.	Nadira Nazrah Abdul Aziz	Malaysian	KMC	4	3	3	5	4	4	3	2	2	1	3	2	3	5	3
249.	Nov Inth Kumar Raja Ram	Malaysian	KMC	4	1	3	5	4	5	3	2	2	3	5	3	3	5	3
250.	Tan Mei Xuan	Malaysian	KMC	4	3	3	5	5	4	2	4	5	3	4	3	2	4	4
251.	Wendy Chen Tyng Tyng	Malaysian	KMC	4	3	3	5	5	4	3	2	3	3	4	3	3	4	3
252.	Oo Cheng Yeow	Malaysian	KMC	4	3	5	5	4	5	2	3	2	4	4	4	5	5	2
253.	Liew Yuan Hwen	Malaysian	KMC	4	4	3	4	5	5	2	3	2	3	3	4	5	1	4
254.	Soo Ki Yang	Malaysian	KMC	4	3	3	5	4	5	2	2	2	1	4	5	3	5	4
255.	Laavania Ganesapiran	Malaysian	KMC	4	3	3	5	5	5	2	2	2	4	3	3	3	4	1
256.	Euscoce Wong	Malaysian	KMC	4	3	3	5	5	5	2	2	2	3	3	3	3	4	5
257.	Nurul Farahnah Binti Mohb Fuad	Malaysian	KMC	4	3	3	3	1	4	2	2	2	1	5	5	3	5	3
258.	Farah Syahida Binti Zubir	Malaysian	KMC	4	3	3	5	4	5	2	2	2	3	4	1	3	4	2
259.	Hazwani Nabihah Binti Basri	Malaysian	KMC	4	3	1	5	5	4	2	2	2	3	4	4	3	4	5
260.	Diana Rosli	Malaysian	KMC	4	4	3	4	4	4	2	2	2	4	3	3	2	4	4

Contd.

Sr. No.	Name	Country	Students University	1	2	3	4	5	6	7	8	9	10	11	12	13	17	20
261.	Logeswari Krishna	Malaysian	KMC	4	3	3	5	5	4	3	2	2	2	5	5	1	5	5
262.	Mahenthrian Gurumoorthy	Malaysian	KMC	4	4	3	4	4	5	3	2	2	3	3	4	3	4	3
263.	Adriana Sigang Langat	Malaysian	KMC	4	3	3	5	4	4	2	2	2	2	5	4	3	5	5
264.	Muhamed Hanif Bin Mohd Deris	Malaysian	KMC	4	4	4	3	5	4	3	5	5	4	5	2	3	4	5
265.	Muhammed Alimin Mat Reffien	Malaysian	KMC	4	4	5	5	4	4	1	2	2	4	4	1	3	4	1
266.	Noor Dalila Binti Beshan	Malaysian	KMC	4	3	3	4	4	4	2	2	2	1	5	2	2	4	5
267.	Syairah Aainaa Binti H Nawawi	Malaysian	KMC	4	4	4	5	5	4	2	2	2	1	5	4	3	4	5
268.	Nor Aidayah Binti Nadzar	Malaysian	KMC	4	3	3	5	5	4	2	2	2	3	4	3	3	3	5
269.	Farah Malinda Bt Md. Kamal F	Malaysian	KMC	4	3	4	5	4	4	2	2	2	4	4	3	4	2	5
270.	Rohilah Binti Halim	Malaysian	KMC	4	3	3	5	5	4	2	2	2	1	4	4	1	4	5
271	Wong Meng Yee	Malaysian	KMC	4	4	3	5	5	4	2	2	2	5	5	2	3	5	4
272	Grace Corrine Khong Yin Leong	Malaysian	KMC	4	3	3	4	5	4	2	3	3	3	5	5	3	4	5
273.	Md. Ibrahim	Maldivian	CMR	5	4	3	4	4	4	2	2	2	4	3	3	2	3	4
274.	Aishath Nafaa Ahmed	Maldivian	CMR	5	5	5	3	4	4	1	3	2	5	3	3	2	3	4
275.	Md. Solah	Maldivian	CMR	5	5	5	5	4	4	4	4	2	2	2	4	4	2	4
276.	Md. Mahid Moosa	Maldivian	CMR	5	5	3	3	5	4	2	4	2	2	2	4	2	2	2
277.	Shifna Mohamed	Maldivian	CMR	2	5	3	4	4	5	4	4	2	3	5	5	5	5	4
278.	Raufuddheen Saeed	Maldivian	CMR	5	3	5	5	4	4	2	4	3	1	5	5	3	4	3
279.	Aishath Sama	Maldivian	CMR	5	5	5	5	4	4	2	2	2	5	5	5	2	2	3
280.	Fathimath Shifaza	Maldivian	CMR	5	5	5	5	4	4	2	5	2	4	4	2	2	4	4

Contd.

Sr. No.	Name	Country	Students University	1	2	3	4	5	6	7	8	9	10	11	12	13	17	20
281.	Ali Hussain	Maldivian	CMR	5	5	3	4	4	4	2	2	2	2	2	2	4	1	2
282.	D.Vickter	Mauritian	DU	2	5	4	5	4	5	2	2	2	4	2	2	5	2	5
283.	Brfhmindrasingh Bheeroo	Mauritian	Mumbai	2	4	4	5	4	5	5	3	4	4	5	5	5	5	4
284.	Bhagwan Luxmi Devi	Mauritian	Mysore	5	3	5	5	4	4	3	2	2	4	5	2	2	4	5
285.	Rojoa Hannah Bibi	Mauritian	Mysore	5	3	2	5	5	2	3	2	3	4	5	2	2	3	5
286.	Hakoon Mushra Begum	Mauritian	Mysore	5	3	2	5	4	4	2	2	2	3	1	3	5	2	5
287.	Shanmouga Prissen P.	Mauritian	KMC	2	3	5	1	4	5	5	5	2	5	4	5	5	5	5
288.	Vanisha Joymungul	Mauritian	Manipal	2	3	4	5	4	5	2	4	5	4	4	5	3	5	3
289.	Farhanaz Jackaria	Mauritian	MAHE	2	4	1	5	5	4	1	5	2	1	5	5	3	2	1
290.	Bundhoo Bhoomita Devi	Mauritian	MIT	2	3	5	5	4	5	5	5	5	5	5	5	3	5	4
291.	Girish Singh Ramlugun	Mauritian	Manipal	2	4	4	5	5	5	1	5	5	4	1	4	5	5	4
292.	Shabana Lalloo	Mauritian	MCODS	2	3	4	4	5	5	2	2	2	3	2	4	5	3	1
293.	Enkhjin Grankhuyay	Mongolian	CMR	5	5	5	5	5	4	4	5	5	1	5	5	5	5	4
294.	Gan-od	Mongolian	CMR	2	3	3	5	5	4	5	3	5	5	5	5	3	5	1
295.	Bayarmaa	Mongolian	CMR	2	3	3	5	5	4	5	4	5	5	5	5	3	5	3
296.	Dashkhuv	Mongolian	CMR	5	2	4	1	5	4	1	2	1	1	5	2	2	4	4
297.	Enkhtsatsral Narabbat	Mongolian	CMR	5	5	4	2	4	4	4	4	2	4	4	4	5	3	4
298.	Zalaa Uul Solongo	Mongolian	Patel University	5	5	4	3	4	5	3	5	5	1	3	4	3	5	5
299.	Rev. A. Shiv Kusala	Myanmar	DU	2	3	4	5	4	5	2	2	4	1	3	3	1	4	3
300.	Myo Win	Myanmar	Mysore	5	3	5	5	4	4	4	5	5	5	4	5	4	5	4

Contd.

Sr. No.	Name	Country	Students University	1	2	3	4	5	6	7	8	9	10	11	12	13	17	20
301.	U. Sandarthiri	Myanmar	Mumbai	2	3	4	5	4	4	2	4	2	1	5	2	2	2	1
302.	U. Ankura	Myanmar	Mumbai	2	3	3	5	4	5	5	4	5	5	5	2	2	2	3
303.	Myo Win	Myanmar	Mysore	5	5	5	4	4	5	5	5	5	4	5	5	4	5	3
304.	Pyi Phyo Aung	Myanmar	MCODS	4	3	4	5	5	4	2	2	2	3	3	4	5	5	2
305.	Uhavara Virere	Namibian	Mysore	5	5	4	3	5	4	2	5	5	2	5	3	3	5	5
306.	Anisha Kansakar	Nepalese	DU	2	5	4	4	5	5	3	3	4	3	5	1	5	5	3
307.	Subrita Sathapit	Nepalese	DU	2	3	4	5	4	5	3	2	3	3	4	5	5	5	3
308.	Bibek Tulachan	Nepalese	CMR	5	5	4	4	4	5	3	4	5	5	5	4	5	5	2
309.	Rajeeb Poudel	Nepalese	CMR	5	5	4	5	4	5	3	4	2	5	3	4	3	5	5
310.	Nabin Kumar Singh	Nepalese	CMR	2	5	3	5	4	4	3	4	5	5	5	3	3	2	2
311.	Amit Kr.Chaudhary	Nepalese	Mysore	5	3	1	1	4	4	2	4	2	3	5	4	5	5	5
312.	Priya Pradhan	Nepalese	Kalina	2	3	5	5	4	4	5	3	4	5	5	2	2	4	4
313.	Anu Lohani	Nepalese	NLS	3	5	5	5	5	5	4	4	4	5	4	4	5	5	3
314.	Femish Acharya	Nepalese	MCODS	2	3	4	5	5	4	2	2	2	4	4	4	5	2	4
315.	Sandeepa Batajoo	Nepalese	MCODS	2	4	5	1	5	4	5	5	2	4	5	4	5	5	4
316.	Ritesh Kumar Shah	Nepalese	BNBIOMS	5	5	5	5	4	4	2	4	2	3	4	2	2	4	5
317.	Kashyap Agrawal	Nepalese	MIOT	2	3	4	5	5	5	3	5	5	5	3	4	3	5	5
318.		Nepalese	Law	3	4	4	4	5	5	5	5	4	5	5	4	4	5	4
319.	Deepak Kumar Das	Nepalese	Patel University	5	5	3	5	4	2	2	5	1	4	3	1	5	5	3
320.	Navin Raj Saroj	Nepalese	Patel University	5	5	3	4	4	5	5	5	1	5	5	3	3	4	3

Contd.

Sr. No.	Name	Country	Students University	1	2	3	4	5	6	7	8	9	10	11	12	13	17	20
321.	Mohan Raj Joshi	Nepalese	Patel University	5	5	3	5	4	4	5	5	5	4	3	2	5	4	4
322.	Saket Kumar Heyal	Nepalese	MCODS	2	3	3	4	5	5	4	1	2	1	5	5	5	5	4
323.	Ramesh Kumar Bhandari	Nepalese	UOP	2	3	3	5	4	5	3	2	2	3	3	2	5	3	5
324.	Sunil Mandal	Nepalese	Patel University	4	5	3	5	4	5	2	5	5	5	5	5	5	5	3
325.	Animesh Kumar	Nepalese	Patel University	5	5	3	5	4	5	2	5	5	3	3	4	5	5	5
326.	Raslam Raj Ragini	Nepalese	Law	2	4	5	5	5	5	5	3	2	2	4	3	5	1	4
327.	Sanjeev Vidyarthi	NRI	Michigan	4	4	4	4	4	3	4	4	4	4	4	5	3	3	4
328.	Sherin Susan Thomas	NRI	CMR	2	3	4	5	5	4	4	4	5	5	5	5	4	5	4
329.	Rema Ashok Varandani	NRI	MCODS	2	3	3	1	5	5	4	2	2	4	3	4	5	4	4
330.	Manmeet Kour Alegh	NRI	MCODS	2	3	3	4	4	5	4	2	2	4	3	4	4	4	2
331.	Nidhi Bakul Kotak	NRI	MCODS	2	3	3	4	4	5	5	5	5	4	3	3	5	5	3
332.	Ubaid Ur Rahman	NRI	MIT	2	4	4	3	4	5	5	5	5	5	5	1	1	5	4
333.	Basil Musaddique Parkar	NRI	Manipal	2	3	4	1	5	4	1	5	5	1	5	2	3	5	4
334.	Geoffrey Dsouza	NRI	Manipal	2	3	5	5	4	5	2	4	5	5	5	2	5	4	3
335.	Zareer Vandrevala	NRI	Manipal	2	3	3	3	4	5	5	5	5	5	5	5	3	4	1
336.	Ausafur Rahman	NRI	Manipal	2	3	5	5	4	5	3	5	2	5	5	5	3	5	3
337.	Ahex Cajetan Mendonca	NRI	Manipal	2	3	3	5	4	5	2	5	5	5	5	5	3	5	5
338.	Nair Anand Damodarankutty	NRI	Manipal	2	4	3	3	4	5	4	1	5	5	4	3	5	5	3
339.	Jithin Mathew George	NRI	Manipal	2	3	4	4	4	5	4	5	5	5	5	3	5	5	3
340.	Shikher Sitoke	NRI	Manipal	2	3	4	5	4	5	5	4	4	4	5	1	3	5	3

Contd.

Sr. No.	Name	Country	Students University	1	2	3	4	5	6	7	8	9	10	11	12	13	17	20
341.	Nelsson X Fernandes	NRI	MIT	2	3	3	4	4	5	2	2	2	1	1	2	4	4	2
342.	Syed Abdul Rahman Fakhri	NRI	Manipal	2	3	4	3	4	5	4	3	2	4	4	2	3	4	5
343.	Michael Victor Thanikkal	NRI	MIT	2	3	3	3	4	5	2	3	2	2	2	3	4	2	1
344.	Sherin Banu	NRI	MIT	2	3	3	4	4	5	5	3	5	5	4	5	3	4	2
345.	Tathagat Yagnik	NRI	MIT	2	3	4	5	5	5	5	3	5	4	5	3	3	4	2
346.	Angad Deep Singh	NRI	MIT	2	3	4	5	5	5	5	1	1	1	5	1	3	5	1
347.	Arun Sunny D'Souza	NRI	MIT	2	3	4	5	5	4	2	2	2	1	3	5	3	1	2
348.	Sooraj Sekhar	NRI	MIT	2	3	3	4	5	4	5	1	1	1	1	1	1	1	2
349.	Roshan George	NRI	MIT	2	4	4	4	5	4	3	2	4	4	3	5	3	5	5
350.	Mekhala Maiti	NRI	MIT	2	3	4	4	4	5	2	5	5	5	4	1	5	5	5
351.	Ritm Susan Alexander	NRI	MIT	2	3	3	5	5	5	2	4	3	5	5	5	3	4	3
352.	Kristel Dacosta	NRI	MIT	2	3	3	5	5	5	2	4	5	5	4	4	3	2	4
353.	Syed Faisal	NRI	Manipal	2	3	4	5	5	4	5	4	4	3	4	3	3	5	4
354.	Jiya James	NRI	Manipal	2	5	3	5	5	4	2	5	5	4	2	1	1	5	5
355.	Mohamed Umair Nasim	NRI	Manipal	2	4	4	5	5	5	5	5	5	5	3	1	4	5	3
356.	Davina Steiphanie Lewis	NRI	Manipal	2	5	5	5	4	5	5	3	5	5	3	4	3	5	4
357.	Vishal Mukesh Mehta	NRI	MCODS	2	3	4	4	5	5	5	5	5	4	4	3	2	1	5
358.	Pearly Anet Jacob	NRI	MCODS	2	3	4	4	5	5	2	2	2	3	2	2	2	1	3
359.	Binita Prabhulal Shah	NRI	MCODS	2	4	4	4	5	5	2	5	5	5	3	2	5	4	3
360.	Abraham Jacob	NRI	Manipal	2	4	3	4	4	5	3	2	1	4	4	2	5	4	2

Contd.

Sr. No.	Name	Country	Students University	1	2	3	4	5	6	7	8	9	10	11	12	13	17	20
361.	Shakeetl Abdobakar Abdulla	NRI	Manipal	2	3	4	5	4	5	2	2	2	5	3	5	3	2	3
362.	Ismail Salin Al. Matrnfi	Omani	ACOU.Hyd.	3	3	5	5	5	3	5	4	4	5	5	5	5	5	4
363.	Yousuf Suleman	Omani	OUS	3	4	5	5	5	3	4	5		5	4	5	4	5	3
364.	Qais Salim Sold Al Salhi	Omani	Nizam	3	5	5	5	5	3	4	4	4	5	5	5	5	5	4
365.	Mohammed Salim Abdullah	Omani		2	3	3	3	4	4	2	3	2	5	5	5	5	5	3
366.	Mohd. Ali Khalid	Palestinian		4	5	4	4	3	5	5	4	4	1	5	1	1	1	3
367.	Ubah Noor Sheik H	Somalian	Nizam	3	3	3	5	5	3	5	5	3	4	5	4	5	5	5
368.	Mohil Ahi Mohel	Somalian	Somalia	3	4	3	5	4	3	1	4	4	1	5	3	4	4	
369.	Athula Samaraleon	Sri Lankan	SIS	3	5	5	5	5	5	3	3	3	4	5	5	1	5	4
370.	Saruhashini Maheswaran	Sri Lankan	Manipal	2	4	5	5	4	5	3	4	4	4	5	5	5	5	4
371.	Chamithvi Rambukwella	Sri Lankan	DU	5	5	4	5	4	5	2	2	2	1	3	3	5	3	4
372.	W.D.S.K. Premasiri	Sri Lankan	DU	5	5	4	5	4	5	2	3	2	4	4	2	5	1	5
373.	Uahesh	Sri Lankan	DU	2	3	3	3	5	5	1	2	2	3	3	2	2	2	4
374.	Surath Chandrasena	Sri Lankan	CMR	5	3	3	5	4	4	4	4	4	3	2	2	1	2	5
375.	G. Dilini S. Lenagala	Sri Lankan	CMR	5	5	5	5	4	4	5	4	2	4	4	3	5	3	5
376.	Nizla Naizer	Sri Lankan	CMR	5	5	5	5	4	4	3	5	4	4	4	3	3	5	4
377.	Niyomi Delwita	Sri Lankan	CMR	5	5	5	5	4	4	3	4	5	4	2	2	2	4	4
378.	Jayathrie Abhisheka G	Sri Lankan	CMR	5	5	5	4	4	4	4	3	2	4	4	5	1	4	4
379.	Deen	Sri Lankan	CMR	5	5	5	5	4	4	3	2	3	3	3	2	2	2	5
380.	Jancy N. Paramanathan	Sri Lankan	KMC	2	4	5	5	4	5	5	5	3	5	5	5	5	5	5

Contd.

Sr. No.	Name	Country	Students University	1	2	3	4	5	6	7	8	9	10	11	12	13	17	20
381.	Nushani Lanka Jayartne	Sri Lankan	KMC	2	3	4	5	4	5	5	5	5	5	5	5	5	5	5
382.	Khalid Abdalla A.	Sudanese	JNU	3	4	1	4	4	5	4	4	4	5	5	5	5	4	3
383.	Ahmed Babiker	Sudanese	JNU	3	4	4	4	4	5	4	4	4	1	4	1	1	4	3
384.		Sudanese	JNU	4	4	3	4	3	5	3	3	3	3	5	5	5	5	5
385.	Adil Ahmed A. Razig	Sudanese	Mumbai	2	5	3	5	5	4	2	4	4	5	5	4	4	5	3
386.	Ali Ahamed Hamid	Sudanese	CMR	2	3	1	1	5	4	2	5	5	1	5	5	3	5	1
387.	Ezzdden Abdelgadir Ah.	Sudanese	Mysore	5	5	2	5	4	4	2	2	2	2	5	5	2	5	4
388.	Elgasim Elmobarak Elkhalifa	Sudanese	Manipal	3	3	5	5	5	3	4	3	5	4	5	4	5	5	3
389.	Eltayib Hassan Ahmed	Sudanese	Patel University	5	3	3	5	5	5	4	2	2	4	4	4	5	5	5
390.	Kifara Fars hasan	Syrian		5	5	1	3	4	4	3	4	2	4	2	5	5	5	1
391.	Hassan	Syrian	BVDU	4	5	5	4	4	4	2	2	2	1	3	4	5	5	5
392.	Faiz	Syrian	BVDU	2	5	3	3	4	1	2	2	1	3	5	3	3	5	5
393.	Nojmedinov Tojiddin	Tajikistan	DU	5	5	1	1	5	5	1	2	1	1	3	1	1	2	3
394.	Upendo Penili	Tanzanian	DU	2	3	5	5	5	5	5	3	5	3	3	5	5	5	3
395.	Deogratue Zoan Mbarara	Tanzanian	CMR	2	3	3	5	5	4	1	4	5	1	4	5	5	5	3
396.	Joanna Sherlin John	Tanzanian	CMR	2	3	3	3	4	4	2	2	2	1	4	2	2	2	3
397.	Lucesia Paul	Tanzanian	CMR	2	3	1	1	1	4	2	5	1	1	4	3	2	4	3
398.	Salum Mohammed	Tanzanian	CMR	2	3	4	5	4	4	5	2	5	5	5	4	3	5	1
399.	Aboud S Jumbe	Tanzanian	Bangalore	5	5	5	5	4	4	2	2	5	5	5	1	2	3	5
400.	Juma C Mbega	Tanzanian	Fergusson	5	5	3	5	4	4	2	2	5	3	3	3	3	5	1

Contd.

Sr. No.	Name	Country	Students University	1	2	3	4	5	6	7	8	9	10	11	12	13	17	20
401.	Jatula Ransibrahmanakul	Thai	CMR	2	5	4	5	4	4	4	4	5	4	4	5	1	1	1
402.	Lunsamrong PhramahaNarong	Thai	CIEFL	5	4	5	4	3	4	4	4	5	5	5	4	5	4	5
403.	Mufaddal Abdulhussan	Thai	Manipal	2	3	5	5	5	5	3	4	2	4	4	3	3	4	4
404.	Tamara Klycheva	Turkmen	NIIT	3	5	5	5	5	3	3	4	4	5	5	5	5	5	4
405.	Abdiwali Mohammed	Ugandan	Nizam	3	4	5	5	5	3	3	4	3	4	5	5	3	5	5
406.	Mama Diev Behzod	Uzbekistan	DU	5	5	3	5	5	5	2	5	2	4	3	3	5	5	5
407.	Behzod Kharajanov	Uzbekistan	BN Bahadur	5	3	3	4	5	4	3	4	4	4	5	3	3	5	4
408.	Bumokhira Sulaymanova	Uzbekistan	Mysore	5	5	4	2	1	4	3	2	2	2	3	3	3	4	4
409.	Shaymardanova Zarema	Uzbekistan	Mysore	5	5	1	1	4	4	3	3	2	2	3	4	4	4	5
410.	Nodira Ba Zaorva	Uzbekistan	Mysore	5	5	1	1	4	4	3	3	2	3	5	5	5	4	5
411.	Ziydulla Abdullah	Uzbekistan	Mysore	5	3	3	4	4	4	2	4	2	4	3	3	5	3	4
412.	Abdusaid A. Abdurashidov	Uzbekistan	Mysore	5	5	4	5	4	4	4	5	4	4	3	4	4	5	2
413.	Uu Thanh Tung	Vietnamese	CMR	5	5	1	2	1	4	1	4	1	1	1	1	1	1	1
414.	Hung	Vietnamese	CMR	2	3	3	4	4	4	1	1	2	1	2	1	1	1	1
415.	Le Thi Vui	Vietnamese		2	3	5	5	5	5	3	2	2	4	5	5	5	1	3
416.	Feras Saleh Ali	Yemeni	JNU	4	4	1	4	1	5	1	4	4	1	5	5	5	4	3
417.	Amear Ahmed Abbas	Yemeni	CIEFL	4	5	5	4	5	3	4	4	4	1	1	1	5	5	1
418.	Airf Ahmed Al Ahdal	Yemeni	CIEFL	5	4	5	5	5	3	3	4	5	4	5	5	4	5	5
419.	Ebrahim AbdullahHezamAl G	Yemeni	Jahnavi	3	3	4	4	4	3	4	4	4	3	4	5	5	5	4
420.	Ameen Saeed Obaid	Yemeni	P.G.Osmania	3	3	4	4	4	3	4	4	5	4	4	5	4	5	4

Contd.

Sr. No.	Name	Country	Students	University	1	2	3	4	5	6	7	8	9	10	11	12	13	17	20
421.	Ali Yahia Ahmed Al.	Yemeni		CIEFL	5	5	4	5	5	3	5	4	5	4	5	5	5	5	5
422.	Mohammed Murshed Ali	Yemeni		ACME	3	4	4	5	5	3	4	5	5	5	5	5	4	5	4
423.	Fair Abdul Sarhan Thabet	Yemeni		J.B.	5	5	5	5	5	3	3	4	4	5	5	5	5	5	2
424.	Afrah Abdullah Ali Alrogheili	Yemeni		Mumbai	4	4	4	5	4	4	2	2	2	5	4	5	3	5	4
425.		Zimbabwean		JNU	4	3	3	4	5	5	3	3	4	1	4	5	1	5	3
426.				NLS	3	4	5	5	5	5	4	5	4	5	4	4	1	5	
427.				Law	3	5	5	5	5	5	5	5	4	1	5	4	1	1	1
428.	Ashin Adel			Fergusson	2	3	5	5	5	4	2	2	2	4	3	3	5	2	3
429.					3	4	5	5	5	5	4	5	4	5	4	4	1	5	4
				Total column	**1338**	**1570**	**1606**	**1826**	**1824**	**1835**	**1310**	**1434**	**1395**	**1409**	**1691**	**1508**	**1570**	**1699**	**1510**
				mean of c	**3.12**	**3.66**	**3.74**	**4.26**	**4.25**	**4.28**	**3.05**	**3.34**	**3.25**	**3.28**	**3.94**	**3.52**	**3.66**	**3.96**	**3.52**

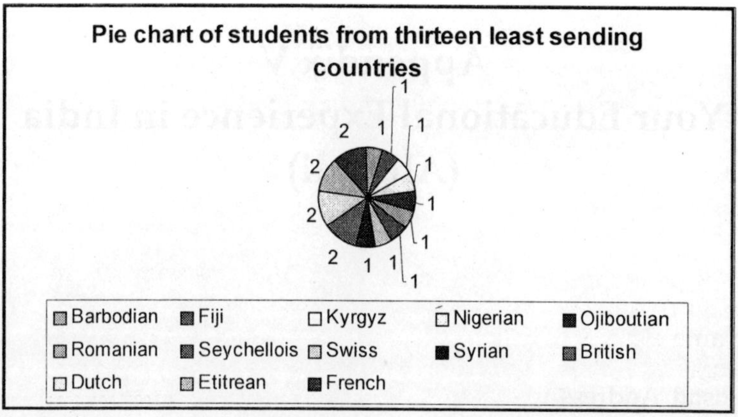
Pie chart of students from thirteen least sending countries
1
2
1
1
2
1
1
2
1
2
1
1
1
Barbodian
Fiji
Kyrgyz
Nigerian
Ojiboutian
Romanian
Seychellois
Swiss
Syrian
British
Dutch
Etitrean
French

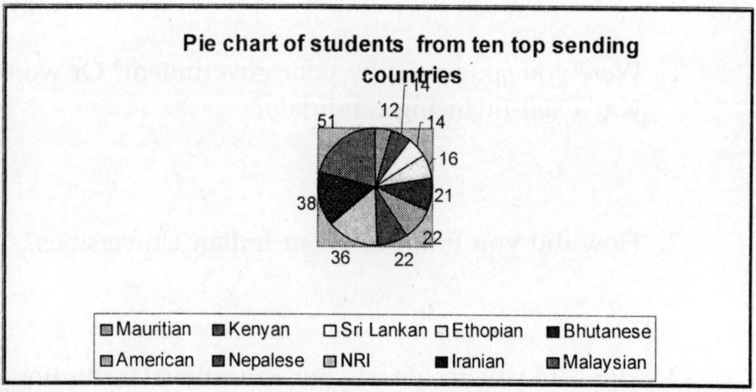
Pie chart of students from ten top sending countries
14
12
51
14
16
38
21
22
36
22
Mauritian
Kenyan
Sri Lankan
Ethopian
Bhutanese
American
Nepalese
NRI
Iranian
Malaysian

Appendix V
Your Educational Experience in India (Alumni)

Name :

Postal Address :

E-mail Address :

Institution in which you studied in India :

Course :

Years :

1. Were you sponsored by your government? Or were you a self-financing candidate?

2. How did you find out about Indian Universities?

3. How did you decide on your educational institution?

4. How did you decide on your course of study?

5. Did you have a preference for a particular town in India? If yes, the reasons for it?

6. Where did you stay in India? In a hostel? Independent accommodation?

7. What were your experiences in the first week of your arrival?

8. How long did you take to settle down physically in India?

9. How long did you take to feel at home?

10. What was the nature of your peer group interaction?

11. What did you get from the course that you pursued? Was it useful on your return? If yes, how?

12. Were you satisfied? Would you have liked some things to be different? If so, what?

13. What are the memories that have remained with you of your stay in India and the course that you pursued?

14. Have you revisited India since then? If yes, what brought you back? If no, was there a reason for it?

15. Did your stay in India in any way help you in the profession that you are currently pursuing?

16. What was the impact of your stay in India on you?

17. Share some important incident or highlights of your stay that stand out in your memory.

18. Would you recommend to others to pursue a course of study in India? If yes, why?

19. If no, what are the reasons?

20. How would you sum up your experience of India as a student?

21. Do you have any suggestions for the institution you attended?

22. Do you have any suggestions for the country in which you were?

23. Does Education/ Study abroad play a role in promoting relations between the countries ? If so how?

    (a) Political (b) Economic and Commercial (c) Cultural

    (d) Scientific and Professional domain (e) Others

24. Your suggestions for promoting cooperation in the field of education between India and your country ?

Weightage : Scaling has been done on a 5-point scale to evaluate the questionnaire for trends.

5 Strongly Agree

4 Agree

3 Disagree

2 Strongly Disagree

1 None of these.

*** The numbers in the head column of Appendix VI refer to the following questions :**

1 Were you sponsored by your Government ? Or were you a self fianancing candidate?

2 How did you find you about Indian Universities?

3 How did you decide on your educational institution?

4 How did you decide on your course of study?

5 Did you have a preference for a particular town in India? If yes, the reason for it?

6 Where did you stay in India? In a hostel? Independent accommodation?

7 What were your experiences in the first week of your arrival?

8 How long did you take to settle down physically in India?

9 How long did you take to feel at home?

10 What was the nature of your peer group interaction?

11 What did you get from the course that you pursued? Was it useful or your term?

If yes, how?

12 Were you satisfied? Would you have liked somethings to be different? If so what?

13 What are the memories that have remained with you of your stay in India and the course you persued?

14 Have you reviisted India since then? If yes, what brought you back? If no, was there a reason for it?

16 What was the impact of your stay in India on you

18 Would you recommed to others a persue a course of study in India? If yes why?

23 Does education/ study abroad play a role in promoting relations between the countries ? If so how?

(a) Political (b) Economical and Commercial
(c) Cultural (d) Scientific and Professional domain
(e) Others

Appendix VI

Study on foreign students (Alumni)

Sr. No.	Name	Country	No student	University	1	2	3	4	5	6	7	8	9	10	11	12	13	14	16	18	23
1	James P. Hare	American	1	VRI	5	4	3	4	5	3	4	4	3	4	4	4	5	5	1	1	5
2	James Mkandawire	Lusaka	1	SIBIT	5	1	5	1	5	1	3	4	3	4	5	3	4	4	5	5	4
3	Selewa Malani	Malawi	1	NIIT	5	4	4	4	5	4	5	4	5	5	5	4	5	5	5	5	5
4	Chatcharavut Chanthananan	Thailand	1	Aryan	2	3	3	3	5	5	2	2	2	4	3	2	5	5	4	4	4
5	Kamalanathan Sappani	Malaysian	3	Karnataka	2	5	4	5	5	5	5	5	5	5	5	2	5	5	5	5	5
6	Amnuay Singh Sukh	NRI	3	Marathawada	2	5	5	5	4	5	5	2	5	5	5	5	5	5	5	5	5
7	Nilam Kumar	Fiji	10	CIH	5	5	5	5	5	5	2	5	5	5	5	3	5	1	5	5	5
8	Crispine Tambo	Zambia	13	CDAC	3	4	4	4	1	3	4	5	5	4	5	4	5	6	5	5	5
9	Prem Chand Bhujanan	Mauritius	22	Ujjain	3	4	4	3	4	5	4	3	3	4	5	5	5	5	5	5	5
10	Epherty Hamakwa	Thailand	57		5	5	5	5	4	4	5	4	4	5	5	5	5	1	1	5	5
11	Darshana Devian Naidu	Fiji		Pune	5	5	5	5	4	4	2	2	2	4	5	2	3	4	5	3	3
12	Jai Prakash Maharaj	Fiji		Bombay	5	1	5	3	5	5	2	5	5	5	5	2	5	2	4	5	5
13	Mridual Prasad	Fiji			2	4	5	5	5	5	5	3	2	4	5	2	5	5	2	1	5
14	Nilam Kumar	Fiji		CIH	5	5	5	5	5	5	4	5	5	5	5	4	5	5	5	5	5
15	Pravir Prasad	Fiji		NCRB	5	5	5	5	5	5	2	2	5	5	5	5	5	5	5	5	5
16	Ram Krishan Reddy	Fiji		Bombay	5	3	3	3	4	5	3	5	2	5	5	1	5	5	2	4	3
17	Seema Sharma	Fiji		DU	5	3	5	5	4	4	2	2	2	5	5	4	5	5	4	5	5
18	Sulasi K. Tamanalevu	Fiji		IKS	5	5	4	5	4	5	2	5	5	5	3	5	5	5	5	5	5
19	Umesh Prasad Sharma	Fiji		CIH	5	5	5	4	4	5	2	5	5	5	5	5	5	1	5	5	5

Sr. No.	Name	Country	No student	Uni-versity	1	2	3	4	5	6	7	8	9	10	11	12	13	14	16	18	23
22	Anitah Aujayeb	Mauritius		DU	3	5	3	5	1	3	4	3	4	4	5	5	5	4	5	5	5
23	Aruna Gobie	Mauritius		DU	5	5	5	5	5	5	4	4	4	5	5	4	5	5	5	5	5
24	Arvin Dijapermal	Mauritius		Bangalore	3	3	4	5	5	3	4	3	3	3	2	4	4	4	4	4	5
25	Atma Bihari	Mauritius		IIT	3	3	3	4	4	3	3	3	3	4	4	3	3	5	4	4	5
26	Basant Vishnu Dutt	Mauritius		Bomay	3	3	3	4	4	3	3	3	3	4	4	3	3	5	4	4	5
27	Chunni	Mauritius		PGI	3	5	4	5	4	5	3	4	4	5	5	5	5	5	5	5	4
28	Dhunputth Satnarayan Singh	Mauritius		DU	3	3	3	4	4	3	3	3	3	4	4	3	3	5	4	4	5
29	Gulshan Sooklall	Mauritius		DU	3	3	4	5	5	3	4	3	3	3	2	4	4	4	4	4	5
30	Kovila Veera Ragoo	Mauritius		Madras	3	5	3	5	1	3	4	3	4	4	5	5	5	4	5	5	5
31	Nirmala Gobin	Mauritius		Delhi	5	5	5	5	5	5	4	4	4	5	5	4	5	5	5	5	5
32	Om Kumar Dawadeen	Mauritius		Jivaji	3	5	3	5	1	3	4	3	4	4	5	5	5	4	5	5	5
33	Rameshwar Tupsy	Mauritius		Bombay	3	5	3	5	1	3	4	3	4	4	5	5	5	4	5	5	5
34	Shanjika Kurji	Mauritius		Pune	3	3	3	4	4	3	3	3	3	4	4	3	3	5	4	4	5
35	Shashi Kumar Baichoo	Mauritius		DU	3	5	3	5	1	3	4	3	4	4	5	5	5	4	5	5	5
36	Shikha Dreepual	Mauritius		Bangalore	3	5	3	5	1	3	4	3	4	4	5	5	5	4	5	5	5
37	Shyam R. Swaven	Mauritius		FMS	3	5	3	5	1	3	4	3	4	4	5	5	5	4	5	5	5
38	Sujata Ramdhari	Mauritius		DU	3	5	3	5	1	3	4	3	4	4	5	5	5	4	5	5	5
39	Thakurdeeal Pawan	Mauritius		ICDS	3	5	3	5	1	3	4	3	4	4	5	5	5	4	5	5	5
40	Venkat Swami Devashley	Mauritius		DU	3	3	4	5	5	3	4	3	3	3	2	4	4	4	4	4	5
41	Vishwadeo Govbin	Mauritius		DU	5	5	5	5	5	5	4	4	4	5	5	4	5	5	5	5	5
42	Win Goodary	Mauritius		DU	3	5	3	5	1	3	4	3	4	4	5	5	5	4	5	5	5
43	Michael Sushil Chandra	NRI		Assam	5	5	5	5	4	5	4	5	5	5	5	5	5	5	5	5	5

Sr. No.	Name	Country	No student	University	1	2	3	4	5	6	7	8	9	10	11	12	13	14	16	18	23
44	Selvamnai K Pillai	NRI		Punjab	4	4	4	4	5	5	5	5	5	1	5	2	5	5	5	5	5
45	Ahrasamot Tyathong	Thailand		Magadh	2	5	5	5	4	5	1	2	4	5	5	5	5	5	5	5	5
46	Bhikkhu Nakorn Khemapali	Thailand		Nalanda	5	5	5	5	4	5	3	5	5	4	5	3	5	5	5	5	5
47	Bhmroong Kham-EK	Thailand		Agra	5	5	5	5	4	5	5	2	5	5	5	5	5	5	5	5	5
48	Bomrdong Kham-Ek	Thailand		Varanasi	4	3	4	3	4	5	5	2	2	3	5	3	5	5	5	5	5
49	Boonchai Choomsanghirun	Thailand		NIFM	4	3	4	5	4	5	2	5	5	4	5	4	5	2	2	5	5
50	Chainarong Klinnoi	Thailand		Pune	3	4	4	1	5	5	3	3	4	1	1	1	5	3	3	5	5
51	Chaiwat Praphanawarat	Thailand		CMC ltd	5	3	1	5	4	2	5	5	5	1	5	4	5	1	3	5	5
52	Chaliw Rodhhein	Thailand		Madras	2	3	3	5	4	5	1	2	2	5	5	5	5	5	1	5	5
53	Chamnong Wongkhong	Thailand		Pune	5	3	1	1	1	1	1	1	1	1	1	1	1	1	1	1	1
54	Chandrqa Chankerajang	Thailand		Punjab	5	5	5	5	5	3	4	5	4	5	5	5	5	5	5	5	5
55	Chanjana Thirapanmethee	Thailand		Pune	3	5	5	5	1	5	3	4	4	5	5	5	5	5	5	5	5
56	Charan Thongkasem	Thailand		Punjab	5	5	5	5	4	5	5	5	5	5	5	5	5	5	5	5	5
57	Chirapat Prapandvidya	Thailand		Baroda	5	5	5	1	4	5	1	5	4	1	5	5	1	5	5	5	5
58	Iddareh Darakai	Thailand			2	3	5	1	5	4	2	2	2	1	4	1	4	1	3	1	1
59	Jaurchet Hongsirisuwan	Thailand		Doon	2	3	3	3	5	5	2	2	2	3	3	2	3	3	3	3	3
60	Kittivut Bnoonprachem	Thailand			2	5	5	1	5	5	2	2	5	1	3	3	5	1	3	3	1
61	Kms. Kotchanop Thipgosai	Thailand		Parliament	5	5	5	5	5	4	4	5	5	4	5	4	5	2	5	5	5
62	Konrawat Timingoon	Thailand		CFTR	5	5	5	5	5	5	2	5	5	5	3	1	4	1	2	5	4
63	Kowit Pimpuang	Thailand		Pune	5	3	3	3	4	5	5	2	5	5	5	5	5	5	5	5	5
64	Mant Paengsai	Thailand		CITD	5	5	5	5	4	5	2	5	5	4	4	3	5	5	5	5	5
65	Nongliksana	Thailand			5	5	5	5	4	5	1	3	5	5	5	5	5	5	5	5	5
66	Ong ard Jitrpom	Thailand		NISIET	5	4	5	5	4	5	3	3	5	4	5	2	3	2	2	2	1

Sr. No.	Name	Country	No student	University	1	2	3	4	5	6	7	8	9	10	11	12	13	14	16	18	23
67	Pharamaha Amnat Pikuntob	Thailand		Nagpur	2	3	4	4	1	5	1	1	1	1	3	1	3	1	4	3	3
68	Phasin Boonsophonpakokn	Thailand		Aryan	2	3	3	3	5	5	2	2	2	4	4	2	5	5	5	5	5
69	Phogsathon Caohasiri	Thailand		Star	2	3	3	3	5	5	2	2	2	3	3	2	4	4	3	4	4
70	Phramaha Daosayam K.	Thailand		Varanasi	2	3	5	3	1	4	2	2	2	1	1	4	1	4	1	1	4
71	Phramaha Maitree Senanan	Thailand		Mysore	2	5	5	3	4	4	5	2	5	5	4	3	5	5	4	2	5
72	Phramaha Som Tipawatana	Thailand		Mysore	2	5	3	3	4	5	5	2	2	5	5	5	5	5	5	5	1
73	Phrasrisitthimuni	Thailand		Delhi	2	5	5	5	4	5	1	2	3	5	5	5	5	5	5	5	5
74	Phrasuthivorayan Cnarong	Thailand		Mysore	5	5	5	5	4	5	4	1	3	5	5	3	4	5	5	5	1
75	Phratherapong Soparak	Thailand		Nagpur	2	3	5	5	4	5	2	2	2	1	3	4	5	5	4	1	4
76	Pibul Nakvanich	Thailand		Pune	5	5	5	5	4	1	1	5	2	3	5	5	5	5	5	5	5
77	Popong Sriithainto	Thailand		Bangalore	2	3	5	1	5	5	4	5	5	1	5	1	1	3	3	3	1
78	Pornpimol Thepjwaski	Thailand		AIIMS	2	3	5	5	4	5	2	5	5	1	5	3	5	5	5	5	5
79	Pramool Sansupa	Thailand		Pune	3	5	5	5	5	3	5	5	5	5	5	5	5	5	4	5	5
80	Pramool Satabantha	Thailand		Baroda	2	5	3	3	4	5	5	2	2	5	3	5	5	5	2	5	5
81	Pranod Nantiyakul	Thailand		Delhi	5	5	5	5	4	5	4	2	5	3	5	1	3	5	5	5	5
82	Pruittiwat Rattanathavesopon	Thailand		Aryan	2	3	3	3	5	5	2	2	2	4	3	2	5	5	4	5	4
83	Samiddhipol Netnimit	Thailand		Banaras	2	3	5	5	4	5	5	2	1	5	5	3	5	3	5	5	1
84	Samniang Leurmsai	Thailand		Banaras	4	3	5	5	4	5	5	3	2	1	5	3	5	5	3	5	1
85	Sanit Sinok	Thailand		Delhi	5	3	5	5	1	5	1	1	5	1	1	3	4	3	1	5	1
86	Sauvakon Jonphongsni	Thailand		sakal	3	5	5	5	5	3	1	4	4	5	5	5	3	5	5	5	5
87	Sombat Mangmeesukhsiri	Thailand		Delhi	2	3	5	5	4	5	2	2	2	5	5	5	5	5	5	5	5
88	Suganya Pandey	Thailand		Shimla	2	1	3	3	5	5	5	2	4	5	1	5	5	2	2	3	5
89	Sunee Musikasil	Thailand		Pune	3	5	3	4	5	5	3	3	3	3	5	5	5	5	5	5	5

Sr. No.	Name	Country	No student	University	1	2	3	4	5	6	7	8	9	10	11	12	13	14	16	18	23
90	Suthastri Glawgitogot	Thailand		Narula	5	1	1	1	5	5	2	2	2	4	5	5	5	3	5	5	5
91	Suttichai Theveenugul	Thailand		Doon	2	3	3	3	5	5	2	2	2	3	3	3	3	3	3	4	4
92	Suwat Khanwong	Thailand		Bombay	3	5	5	5	5	5	3	4	5	4	5	5	1	3	5	5	5
93	Tanistha Dansilp	Thailand			5	2	4	5	5	5	5	5	5	5	5	5	5	5	1	5	5
94	Tewat Bunpa	Thailand		Aryan	2	3	3	3	5	5	2	2	2	4	3	2	5	5	5	5	5
95	Thivavath Issarangure	Thailand		Magadh	5	3	3	5	5	5	5	5	2	3	5	3	3	1	5	1	3
96	Thongbai Dhiranandanklura	Thailand		Punjab	3	3	3	5	5	5	3	3	3	3	5	5	5	3	5	5	5
97	Vanchai Chunrachakul	Thailand		Pune	3	5	3	5	5	3	3	3	3	4	5	5	5	3	5	5	5
98	Whirach Thirapanhcthee	Thailand		Pune	3	5	5	5	5	4	3	4	4	5	5	5	5	5	5	5	5
99	Yaowapa Maneechai	Thailand		ISI Kolkata	5	1	5	5	5	5	5	1	5	5	5	4	5	1	1	5	5
100	Yuen Paraken	Thailand		IIT	5	5	5	5	5	5	3	3	3	4	5	5	5	5	5	5	5
101	Alick Mwamza	Zambia		IIRS	5	5	4	5	5	5	4	4	4	5	5	4	4	4	4	5	5
102	Andrew Tembo	Zambia		EDI	5	5	5	5	3	5	4	4	4	5	5	5	5	4	5	5	5
103	Brigen Muchopa	Zambia		Nasik	5	1	4	4	5	5	4	4	4	4	5	5	4	4	5	5	5
104	Duncan Moyo	Zambia			5	5	5	5	3	4	4	4	4	5	5	5	4	3	5	5	4
105	Elias Lungu	Zambia		IIMC	5	5	5	5	4	5	5	4	4	5	5	5	5	5	5	5	5
106	Evelyen Mwamba	Zambia		SIBIT	5	4	4	5	5	4	3	3	3	4	5	5	5	4	4	5	5
107	Jeorge Mbesla	Zambia			5	4	5	5	1	4	4	4	4	4	5	4	5	4	5	5	5
108	Mascka Najapaw	Zambia		IAMR	5	5	4	1	1	5	4	3	3	5	5	4	4	3	5	5	5
109	Rosaira M Lubumbashi	Zambia		IIMC	5	5	4	4	4	5	2	3	3	4	5	4	5	4	4	5	5
110	Siamemoulen	Zambia		NIESBUD	5	5	4	5	5	5	4	6	6	5	5	5	5	6	5	5	4
111	Spriiana Banda	Zambia		NIIT	5	4	5	5	5	4	3	3	4	5	5	5	4	4	5	5	4
112	Vitarianah Moonga	Zambia		ICM	5	3	4	5	5	4	4	5	5	5	5	4	5	4	1	1	1
			Total of column		**416**	**451**	**458**	**477**	**442**	**485**	**367**	**370**	**409**	**443**	**498**	**434**	**502**	**453**	**467**	**497**	**493**
			Mean of column		**3.71**	**4.03**	**4.09**	**4.26**	**3.95**	**4.33**	**3.28**	**3.30**	**3.65**	**3.96**	**4.45**	**3.88**	**4.48**	**4.04**	**4.17**	**4.44**	**4.40**

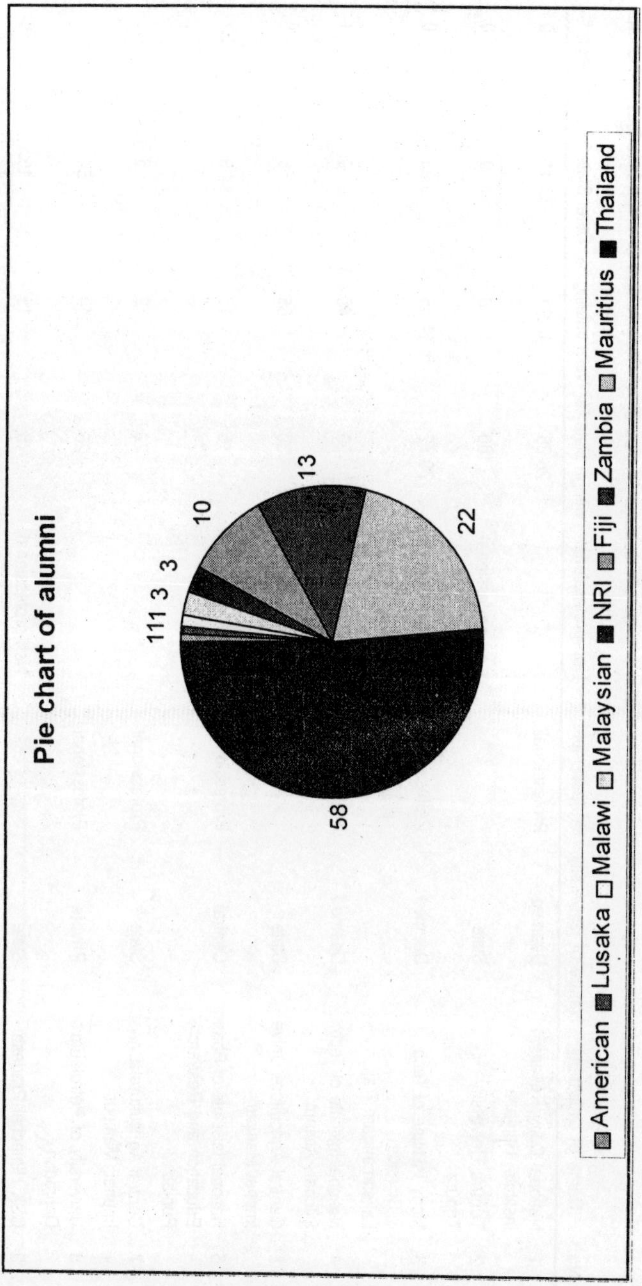
Pie chart of alumni
58
111
3
3
10
13
22
American
Lusaka
Malawi
Malaysian
NRI
Fiji
Zambia
Mauritius
Thailand

Appendix VII
Basic Facts of Student Diversity

Sr No.	Name of University	Nature of University	Subject		Percentage Distribution of Geographical Diversity at various Institutions U G level			
			Professional	Non-professional	with in state %	Neighbouring %	Other State %	Foreign %
1	National Dairy Research Institute, Haryana	Deemed	Professional		26.66	40.93	32.41	0
2	Tripura University Tripura	State		Non-professional	100	0	0	0
3	Mody Institute of Tech & Science Lakshmangarh Raj.	Deemed	Professional		79.72	14.35	5.93	0
4	National Institute of Tech. Silchar, Assam	Deemed	Professional		50	49	0	1
5	Central Agriculture Unive. Imphal Manipur	State		Non-professional	30	65	5	0
6	National Inistitute of Pharm. Education and Research Punjab	Central	Professional		5	10	84.9	0.1
7	Central Agricultural Univ. Imphal, Manipur	State	Professional		22	72	6	0
8	University of Petroleum Dehradun	Private	Professional		26	10	64	0
9	CSK Himachal Pradesh Krishi Vishvavaidyalaya	State		Non-professional	70	15	15	0

Sr No.	Name of University	Nature of University	Professional	Non-professional	with in state %	Neighbouring %	Other State %	Foreign %
			Subjects		Percentage Distribution of Geographical Diversity at various Institutions UG level			
10	Swami Ramanand Teerath Marathwada Univ. Nanded	State	Professioanl		95.61	2.06	2.33	0
11	Sardar Vallabh Bhai Patel University of Agriculture Technology Meerut	State		Non-professional	72	0	25	3
12	National Institute of Tech. Jamshedpur	Deemed	Professional		50	0	49.5	0.5
13	National Brain Research Cen. Manesar, Haryana	State	Professional		2	48	50	0
14	Manipal Academy of Higher Education	Deemed	Professional		97	0	0	3
15	Birla Insitute of Technology Ranchi	Deemed	Professional		39.5	53.5	0	7
16	Rajiv Gandhi Univesity Rono Hills Itanagar	State		Non-professional	83.1	16.9	0	0
17	Integral University Kursi Road, Lucknow	Private	Professional		97.35	2.48	0.17	0
18	Swami Vivekananda Yoga Anusandhana Samsthana Karnataka	Deemed	Professional		42	21	24	13
19	Tamil Nadu Open University Chennai	State		Non-professional	97.34	2.56	0.1	0

			Percentage Distribution of Geographical Diversity at various Institutions					
			Subjects		UG level			
Sr No.	Name of University	Nature of University	Professional	Non-professional	with in state %	Neighbouring %	Other State %	Foreign %
20	North Eastern Hill Univ. Shillong	State		Non-professional	79	20	1	0
21	Jadavpur University Kolkata	State		Non-professional	98	1	1	0
22	Visvesvaraya National Institute of Tech. Nagpur	State		Non-professional	50	0	49.5	0.5
23	Rashtrasant Tukadoji Mah. Nagpur University	State		Non-professional	93	2	4	1
24	Dibrugarh University Assam	State		Non-professional	95	5	0	0
25	Dr. B. R. Ambedkar National Institute of Technology	Deemed	Professional		50	0	50	0
26	Guru Jambheshwar Univ. Hisar	State	Professional		90	10	0	0
27	Tamil University Thanjavur	State	Professional		99	0	0	1
28	Fakir Mohan Univesity Balasore Orissa	State	Professional		96.78	3.22	0	0
29	Avinashilingam Institute Home Science and Higher Coimbatore	State		Non-professional	92	6	2	0

Sr No.	Name of University	Nature of University	Subjects		Percentage Distribution of Geographical Diversity at various Institutions UG level			
			Professional	Non-professional	with in state %	Neighbouring %	Other State %	Foreign %
30	Rashitriya Sanskrit Vidyapetha Tirupati	State		Non-professional	50	30	20	0
31	Kanpur University	State		Non-professional	95	5	0	0
32	Goa University	State		Non-professional	91	7	2.5	0.5
33	Acharya N. G. Ranga Agri. University Hyderabad	State	Professional		85	0	15	0
34	Dhirubhai Ambani Inst. Of Inf. And Comm. Tech Gujarat	Private		Non-professional	10	0	90	0
35	Fakir Mohan Univesity Balasore	State		Non-professional	99	0	1	0
36	Sri Sathya Sai Institute of Higher Learning	State	Professional		57	14	28.84	0.16
37	Veer Kunwar Singh University Ara	State	Professional		99	1	0	0
38	Bhavnagar University Gujrat	State	Professional		100	0	0	0
39	Indira Kala Sangit Vishvadya Kharagarh	State	Professional		55	31	14	0
40	Kuvempu University	State	Professional		99	0.68	0.3	0.02
41	Sambalpur University Orissa	State		Non professional	60	20	18	2

			Subjects		Percentage Distribution of Geographical Diversity at various Institutions UG level			
Sr No.	Name of University	Nature of University	Professional	Non-professional	with in state %	Neighbouring %	Other State %	Foreign %
42	Manipur University Manipur	State		Non-professional	100	0	0	0
43	Solapur University Maharashtra	State		Non-professional	99	1	0	0
44	Devi Ahilya Vishwavidyalaya Indore	State		Non-professional	70	24	5	
45	Swami Ramanand Teerth Marathwada University Nanded	State		Non-professional	95.61	2.04	2.35	0
46	Shivaji University Vidyanagar	State		Non-professional	98	1.5	0.5	0
47	North Maharashtra University Jalgaon	State		Non-professsional	99.74	0.26	0	0
48	Jawaharlal Nehru Tech. University, AP	State	Professional		100	0	0	0
49	Kakatiya University Warangal, AP	State	Professional		100	0	0	0
50	Dibrugarh University Assam	State	Professional		95	5	0	0
51	National Institute of Tech. Mahatma Gandhi Avenue Durgapur	State		Non-professional	50	8.2	41.76	0.04

Sr No.	Name of University	Nature of University	Subjects: Professional	Subjects: Non-professional	UG level: with in state %	UG level: Neighbouring %	UG level: Other State %	UG level: Foreign %
					Percentage Distribution of Geographical Diversity at various Institutions			
52	Guru Nanak Dev Univesity Amitsar	State		Non-professional	71	20	6	3
53	University of North Bengal West Bengal	State		Non-professional	97.8	2.18	0.02	0
54	Vellore institute of Tech. Tamilnadu	Deeemed	Professional		22.7	34.63	42.63	0.04
55	DDU Gorakhpur University Gorakhpur	State		Non-professional	95	4	1	0
56	Banasthali Vidyapith Rajasthan	Deemed		Non-professional	34.4	36.25	25.69	3.66
57	Amrita Vishwa Didyapeetham	Deemed		Non-professional	69	6	10	15
58	National Institute of Tech. Himachal	Deemed	Professional		50	0	50	0
59	Shri Lal Bahadur Shastri Rashtriya Sanskrit Vidyapith New Delhi	Deemed		Non-professional	8.72	89.78	1.5	0
60	Deccan College Pune	Deemed		Non0professsional	44.4	6.34	32.66	16.6
61	Meenakshi Academy of Higher Education & Research Chennai	Deemed		Non-professional	69.18	25.56	0	5.26

Sr No.	Name of University	Nature of University	Subjects: Professional	Subjects: Non-professional	Percentage Distribution of Geographical Diversity at various Institutions UG level: with in state %	Neighbouring %	Other State %	Foreign %
62	Rashtriya Sanskrit Vidyapith Tirupati	Deemed		Non-professional	50	30	20	0
63	International institute of information Techonology Hyderabad	Deemed	Professional		54.35	0	45.65	0
64	Indian Veterinary Research Institute Izatnagar UP	Deemed	Professional		26	22.96	51	0.04
65	Sardar Vallabhbai National Institute of Technology Gujrat	Deemed	Professional		50	0	50	0
66	Symbiosis International Educational Centre Pune	Deemed	Professional		28	0	67	5
67	Pravara Institute of Medical Sciences Maharastra	Deemed	Professional		80	12	8	0
68	Narsee Monjee Institute of Management Studies Mumbai	Deemed	Professional		48	12	40	0
69	Dr. Yashwant Parmar Univ. of Horticulture Solan, HP	State		Non-professional	60	22	9	9
70	Guru Jambheshwar Univ. Hisar	State	Professional		93	5	2	0

Sr No.	Name of University	Nature of University	Subjects Professional	Non-professional	Percentage Distribution of Geographical Diversity at various Institutions UG level with in state %	Neighbouring %	Other State %	Foreign %
71	Dharmsinh Desai University Gujrat	State	Professional		99	0.7	0.3	0
72	Maharashtra University of Health Science Nashik	State	Professional		85	0	15	0
73	SRI Venkateswara Institute of Medical Sciences Tirupati	State	Professional		100	0	0	0
74	University of Kota Kota	State	Professional		98	1.5	0.5	0
75	West Bengal Universisty of Technology Kolkata	State	Professional		100	0	0	0
76	Maulana Azad National Urdu University	Central		Non-professional	75	20	5	0
77	Assam Agricultural Univ. Jorhat	State		Non-professional	59	26	15	0
78	Kurukshetra University Kurukshetra	State		Non-professional	65	22	5	8
79	Dr. Babasaheb Ambedkar Open University Gujarat	State		Non-professional	100	0	0	0
80	Nirma University Ahmedabad	Private	Professional		100	0	0	0
81	Indian Institute of Foreign Tra. New Delhi	Deemed	Professional		67	7	26	0

			Percentage Distribution of Geographical Diversity at various Institutions					
			Subjects		UG level			
Sr No.	Name of University	Nature of University	Professional	Non-professional	with in state %	Neighbouring %	Other State %	Foreign %
82	SRM institute of Science and Technology Tamilnadu	Deemed	Professional		75	13	10	2
83	Institute of Technology and Sciences Tamil Nadu	Deemed	Professional		68.86	19.23	10.55	1.36
84	Jain Vishva Bharati Institute Rajasthan	Deemed	Professional		94.67	4.56	0.77	0
85	Dr. B. R. Ambedkar National Institute of Technology Jalandhar	Deemed	Professional		50	0	50	0
86	University of Madras Chennai	State	Professional		90	7	2	1
87	Jamia Hamdard New Delhi	Deemed	Professional		23	34	35	8
88	Jaypee Institute of Inf. Tech. Noida	Deemed	Professional		44	25	27	4
89	Bharathidasan Univesity Tamilnadu	State	Professional		97.44	2	0.33	0.23
90	Madurai Kamaraj University Tamil Nadu	State	Professional		69	0	31	0
91	Chaudhary Charan Univesity Hisar	State		Non-professional	85	5	10	0

Sr No.	Name of University	Nature. of University	Subjects Professional	Non-professional	Percentage Distribution of Geographical Diversity at various Institutions UG level with in state %	Neighbouring %	Other State %	Foreign %
92	Govind Ballabh pant University of Agri. & Tech. Uttaranchal	State	Professional		90	5	4.5	0.5
93	Jawaharlal Nehru Univesity New Delhi	Central		Non-professional	20	5	70	5
94	Dr. Ram Manohar Lohia Avadh University, Faizabad	State		Non-professional	70	25	5	0
95	Indira Gandhi Insitute of Development Research Mumbai	Deemed	Professional		7	0	93	0
96	National Institute of Tech. Calicut	Deemed	Professional		50	7	40	3
97	Univesity of Mysore Mysore	State	Professional		40	30	20	10
98	Gujarat Vidyapith Ahmedbad	Deemed		Non professional	100	0	0	0
99	University of Rajasthan Jaipur	State		Non-professional	95	0	5	0
100	Thapar Institute of Eng.&Tech. Patiala	Deemed	Professional		71	12	14	3
101	Dev Sanskrit Vishvavidhya Uttaranchal	State		Non-professional	12.4	43.6	42.1	1.9

Sr No.	Name of University	Nature of University	Subjects		Percentage Distribution of Geographical Diversity at various Institutions UG level			
			Professional	Non-professional	with in state %	Neighbouring %	Other State %	Foreign %
102	Dev Sanskrit Vishwavidhalaya	State	Professional		12.2	43.8	42.1	1.9
103	Bidhan Chandra Krishi Viswavidyalaya West Bengal	State		Non-professional	85	0	15	0
104	Jamia Millia Islamia New Delhi	Central		Non-professional	32	29.4	37.6	1
105	Tamil University Tamil Nadu	State		Non-professional	99	0	0	1
106	Kannada University Hampi Vidyaranya	State		Non-professional	100	0	0	0
107	Shri Mata Vaishno Devi University, J & K	State		Non-professional	79.6	3.7	16.7	0
108	Bangalore University Bangalore	State		Non-professional	75	5	15	5
109	Punjabi University Patiala	State	Professional		96.64	2	0.41	0.95
110	Tezpur University Assam	Central		Non-professional	82.39	0	17.61	0
111	Kannur University Kerala	State	Professional		95	5	0	0
112	Rajiv Gandhi Proudyogiki Vishwavidyalaya M.P	State	Professional		75	15	5	5

Percentage Distribution of Geographical Diversity at various Institutions

Sr No.	Name of University	Nature of University	Subjects: Professional	Subjects: Non-professional	UG level: with in state %	UG level: Neighbouring %	UG level: Other State %	UG level: Foreign %
113	Bharathiar University Coimbatore	State		Non-professional	69	31	0	0
114	Punjab University Chandigarh	State		Non-professional	22.78	27.41	44.81	5
115	Tilak Maharashtra Vidyapith Pune	State		Non-professional	90.01	4.84	2.76	2.39
116	Kalinga Institute of Industrial Technology, Orissa	Deemed	Professional		20	50	30	0
					8020.95	**1481.12**	**1937.28**	**161.65**

1	Mean of students within states	69.15
2	Mean of students of neighboring states	12.77
3	Mean of students of other state	16.70
4	Mean of students of foreign countries	1.39

Source: Survey done by Mr. Pawan Aggarwal

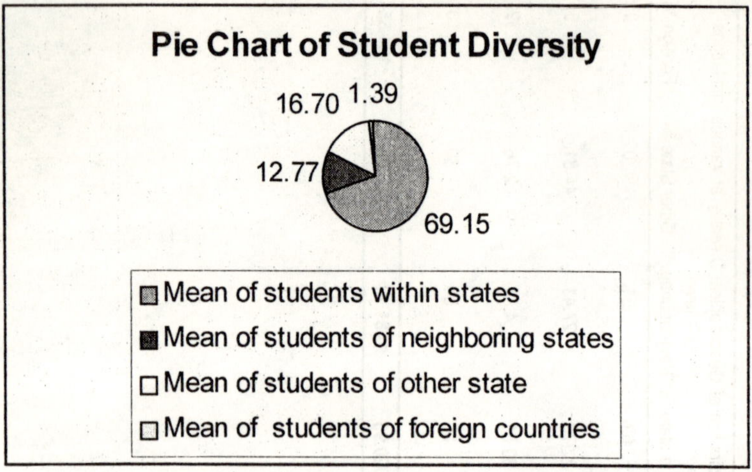
Pie Chart of Student Diversity
16.70
1.39
12.77
69.15
Mean of students within states
Mean of students of neighboring states
Mean of students of other state
Mean of students of foreign countries

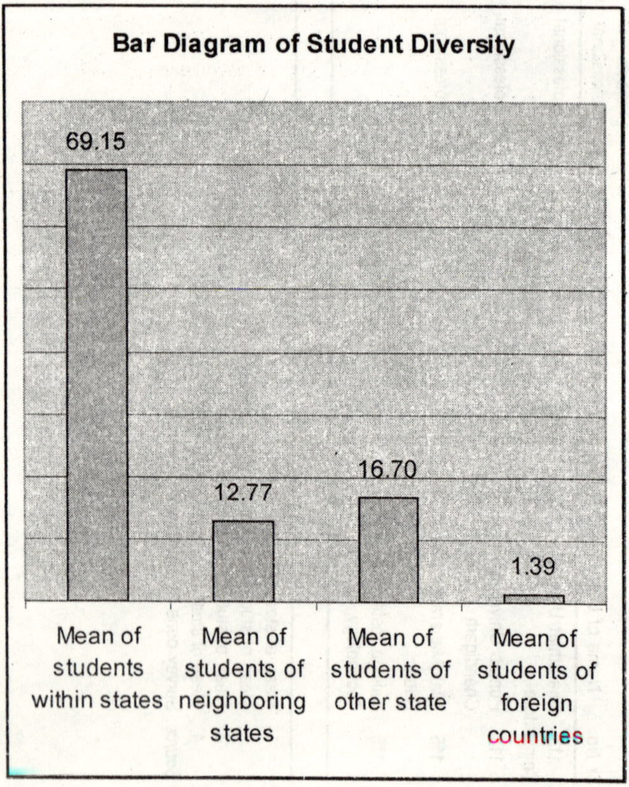
Bar Diagram of Student Diversity
69.15
12.77
16.70
1.39
Mean of students within states
Mean of students of neighboring states
Mean of students of other state
Mean of students of foreign countries

Index

B

C

D

E